PENGUIN BOOKS

TWENTIETH-CENTURY
BOOK OF THE DEAD

Gil Elliot was born in Kilmacolm, Scotland, in 1931. He has worked in business and market research in between spells at Glasgow and more recently Sussex University.

Twentieth Century Book of the Dead is the first of three books. The second, *Lucifer*, is a biography of the devil; the third, *City of Dreams*, a projected study of the 'the paradisial consciousness'.

Twentieth-Century Book of the Dead

GIL ELLIOT

PENGUIN BOOKS

Penguin Books Ltd, Harmondsworth, Middlesex, England
Penguin Books Australia Ltd, Ringwood, Victoria, Australia

—

First published by Allen Lane The Penguin Press 1972
Published in Penguin Books 1973

—

Copyright © Gil Elliot, 1972

—

Made and printed in Great Britain by
Hazell Watson & Viney Ltd, Aylesbury, Bucks
Set in Monotype Plantin

FOR HELEN

*My grateful thanks are due to
Edward Luttwak and Oliver Caldecott for
helping to bring this book into being,
to Joan Westcott for suggesting many
helpful amendments to the text and to
Mira Coopman for her encouragement
and support of the book.*

CONTENTS

CONTENTS

BOOK THREE

VALUES: NEGATIVE AND POSITIVE

1

INTRODUCTION:
DEATH OF THE PEOPLE

HISTORY AND THE DEAD

THE number of man-made deaths in the twentieth century is about one hundred million. Men, women and children each make up a substantial proportion of that total.

A more accurate figure would depend on the particular definition of 'man-made death'. But in any reasonable meaning of the phrase it cannot be less than eighty million; it is unlikely to be much more than a hundred and fifty million.

To set such a figure against the scale of violence in previous times involves the difficulties of comparing like periods and of allowing for population increase. However, every attempt to do so shows the twentieth century to be incomparably the more violent period.

It is possible – in my view, certain – that in a future perspective this explosion of human lives will be seen as the significant 'history' of our period. Yet the events which have accumulated to form this history – millions upon millions of individual violent deaths – are often recorded in historical footnotes or in quickly read and rather meaningless statistics. Many written histories don't even mention them, although dealing in detail with the events that led up to and followed them.

A historian might record the 'cost' of a campaign in China in the 1930s (or Biafra in the 1960s) as follows:

Casualties (deaths)	
Military	Civilian
29,638	Unknown, possibly several million

Since the only records of casualties are kept by those who incur and cause them, the likeliest source of such figures would be a military commander. However confused and inaccurate the methods of his units in counting the dead and wounded, they would produce a tidy official figure because that is what is required of them. The civilian dead would be, for him, marginal to his main interest and for them he would be content to return an 'unofficial estimate'. The historian knows very well that several million deaths must be a phenomenon of enormous significance. Recorded in the above form, however, they appear as a casual effect of some larger event. The impression is encouraged by the vagueness of the figure and its unofficial (unreal?) status. It certainly does not have the crisp reality of that '29,638'. The reader might even have an unconscious admiration for the humanity of these last three digits – every last man counted! – although in fact they are the product of bureaucratic necessity. And, of course, it is perfectly easy to visualize the brave soldiers falling in battle. But what exactly is a Chinese or Biafran peasant, and how can one guess at the manner of his or her death – did he die of starvation or disease? did he get in the way of the guns?

This lack of historical focus on those who get themselves killed is to be found also in the campaign and other histories of the two world wars. Many of these are remarkable for an almost total absence of human beings. They describe the struggles of the tanks, guns, battalions, supplies, barbed wire, divisions. The phrase 'hideous carnage' – compulsively used to denote the effects of battle – curiously underscores the absence of the human image by mingling its meaty flavours with the smell of cordite, the shapes of twisted metal, the messes of mud and masonry. The dead take their place, along with burnt-out tanks and empty petrol cans, among the waste material of history.

The common effect of these tendencies is to perpetuate a 'cost' or 'balance-sheet' view of casualties – appropriate to small military operations – in areas where violent death has occurred on a vast scale. The taking of life loses its meaning, the significance of scale is deprived of any value, and human beings are marginalized in the record of human affairs.

In case it is thought that war historians are especially callous, it is worth pointing to a widespread degeneracy in this respect in writings of the last fifty years. Some of the most notable pacifist works of the period are equally short on human beings. There seems to have been a general lack of confidence in the nature of the species, an embarrassed reluctance to give it more than passing mention.

Recently there have been some signs that the pseudo-scientific attitudes which obscure the human image from expression are being discredited. At the same time, the closing-in of the world communications network and the pressures of public opinion have made newspapers precise in their recording of casualties. The horrors of war have been exposed on television. Excellent and compassionate war histories have been written.

It seems, however, that there is a limit to the extent to which the reality of large-scale violent death can be comprehended. Accurate casualty figures are quickly publicized, the death of a child in Viet-Nam is described in depth of horror. Such information may cause a salutary sense of shock; but what follows shock? Statistics and horror, it seems, are not enough. Horror makes death vivid to the observer. Figures convey a kind of truth. But they cannot communicate the moral value of a single death, nor the moral difference between ten thousand and two million deaths.

Many people who have read accounts of concentration camp atrocities may have noticed in themselves certain confused reactions, including a kind of perverted pleasure. Those who have such feelings unconsciously and without examining them may simply develop a pornographic relish for the material. Others may have a lively sense of conniving at the atrocities which perhaps leads to guilty rationalizations such as, 'Everyone is capable of such actions. Man is fundamentally barbarous' – an even more demoralizing effect than that of the man who simply adds sadistic horror to his range of mental pleasures!

The psychologist might legitimately adduce all sorts of guilty reasons for such a reaction. But there is one innocent condition which seems basic to the issue, and that is simply the ordinary structure of language.

When a child comes running to us crying, 'Johnny hit me!' we are often reluctant to sympathize. The verbal structure of the sentence gives an existential dignity to Johnny. The word 'hit' reflects his active and vital existence. Before considering 'me' – the victim – we shall want to know, how badly is he hurt, what did he do to provoke Johnny. In order to dignify the victim's case we have to construct a moral context for it.

The child who is *playing* at being a victim is often more alive to his own interests. 'Bang-bang,' come the words of the shot. 'You've deaded me!' he shrieks, dramatically falling to the ground. By using a fantasy-verb which reflects the existence of the sufferer, the child claims an existential dignity greater than that of his persecutor.

But in real life verbs usually assert the existence of the subject not the object. Language carries a bonus for the doer. Unless the existence of the sufferer is strongly realized, in moral or material terms, we tend to identify with the active-principle embodied in the actor. If the active-principle adheres not in human beings but in guns – as it often does in battle histories as well as cheap thrillers – then we might find ourselves identifying with agents of pure destruction. And not because of sado-masochistic impulses or phallic inducement, but simply because of the moral innocence and the innocent bias of language. The existential significance of the sufferer must, like justice, be demonstrated. It cannot be assumed.

Techniques of expression do exist, of course, for bringing the existence of the sufferer, or the oppressed, into focus. Any method that is purely moralistic or purely materialistic is probably calculated to do violence to the interest it advocates. Moralizers for example sometimes impute to victims qualities of goodness and innocence they do not possess, or assume that there is something inherently 'noble' about their suffering. Marxism asserts the material existence of the oppressed, but its technique of pointing to concealed motives on the part of oppressors can have dubious results. A neo-Marxist informs us, for instance, that 'tolerance is oppression'. Language at that simple level of distortion is itself an instrument of violence.

It should be emphasized however that material effects can

alter our existential view of the sufferer. A plague victim of the Middle Ages was often regarded as a bringer of evil, even a sinner by association. Today he would be associated with hospitals, medicines, the possibility of cure. Material improvements have created a new moral context for his suffering.

What is the moral context in which we should see those killed by violence? There exists a view that one violent death has the same moral value as a thousand or a million deaths. Presumably 'moral value', in this view, is kept in jars of concentrated essence on the shelves of philosophers, or in the divine pantry. The killer cannot add to his sin by committing more than one murder. However, every *victim* of murder would claim, if he could, that his death had a separate moral value. Thus there is an accretion of moral significance in quantity of deaths. There is no doubt that this is difficult for the imagination to compute. After a certain stage in assimilating casualties, the rest seems an indigestible piling-on of horror and numbers. So long as the moral significance of scale is not understood, only the crudest relationships can be made in the discussion of macro-violence: the Nazis were wicked, Stalin was a monster, and so forth. How then are we to understand scale?

As we have seen, it is absurd to look upon the hundred million or so man-made deaths of the twentieth century as the 'cost' of conflict, as though they were the casualty returns of a field commander. They are more directly comparable with the scale of death from disease and plague which was the accepted norm before this century. Indeed, man-made death has largely replaced these as a source of untimely death. This is the kind of change that Hegel meant when he said that a quantitative change, if large enough, could bring about a qualitative change. The quality of this particular change becomes clear if we connect the present total of deaths with the scale of death inherent in the weapons now possessed by the large powers. Nuclear strategists talk in terms of hundreds of millions of deaths, of the destruction of whole nations and even of the entire human race. The moral significance is inescapable. If morality refers to relations between individuals, or between the individual and society, then there can be no more fundamental moral issue than the continuing survival of individuals and societies. The scale of man-made death is the central moral as well as material fact of our time. The 'historical necessity' of Marxist materialism as well as the individual morality of Christianity must bow to its significance.

If we have found a moral context for those vast numbers killed by violence, this will not be greatly meaningful unless we can bring the dead into existential focus. As we have seen, there has been a historical reluctance to do so in the absence of the human image from written history. There is a further and more persistent barrier in the very nature of language.

We may begin to overcome these difficulties if we compare the scale of man-made death with the scale on which a modern nation operates and lives. The obvious reason for the comparison is simply that the figure of a hundred million represents the size in population of a large modern nation, and as a familiar image it may help us to visualize the scale and complexity of man-made death. Just as we can observe the life of a nation and character-ize it as in some ways made up of like behaviour and in some ways of variant behaviour, so, if we think of a nation of the dead, we may begin to comprehend the varieties of types of violence, of people and of moral entities, which form it as a whole, and to discover by comparing these the true common factors which make it a nation.

The nation of the dead is not a mystical, but a finite histor-ical concept, for it has a limited number of alternative desti-nies.

Either the nation of the dead will come to be seen as an isolated phenomenon of the twentieth century – in which case history will want to know more and more about its make-up and characteristics.

Or it will grow by fits and starts as an ever-increasing menace to the idea of civilization – and the sooner history identifies the nature of that threat the better.

Or, through some cataclysm in the future it will swell in numbers to obliterate in significance any nation of the living. In that case it will be the final phenomenon of our history.

There are no other possibilities.

BOOKS OF THE DEAD

BOOKS of the dead are in general very upbeat in tone. At least this is true of the *Egyptian Book of the Dead* and the *Tibetan Book of the Dead*. It is not surprising that they should be so, for after all they are offering the key to a life after death. A cheerful prospect. The present work does not propose to offer any such liberation from known reality. That is unimaginative, but it is part of my conception of the truth. Indeed, my prospectus offers little for those facing what might nowadays be called 'private' or 'civil' death. The individual is free to indulge in whatever thoughts he likes – gloomy or bland – on the subject of his own death. He has a good lifetime to think about it, so why should he be dominated by one interpretation, why shouldn't he run the gamut of emotions? If he belongs to an advanced industrial society, he as like as not will live to over seventy. Medicine and public health have largely freed him from the terrors of disease and plague, from seeing his children carried off in their weakness. Death is the end of a life, not an enemy that constantly threatens to interrupt it. What vistas of mournful cypresses he chooses for his death – purple brasses tuning faint glories in the melancholy stir of dark leaves! – are his own affair. He may see it as a relief from gas bills. He may grieve for others but never feel his own. It is not private death we are concerned with here, but the reality and threat that carry people off into those public deaths of battle slaughter, massacre and slow, cruel siege.

The ancient books of the dead were in a sense concerned with public death. For the afterlife was an extension of the public domain. It was part of the official ambience of society. Our societies are dedicated to the preservation and care of life. Official concern ceases at death, the rest is private. Public death was first recognized as a matter of civilized concern in the nineteenth century, when some health workers decided that untimely death was a question between men and society, not between men and God. Infant mortality and endemic disease became matters of social responsibility. Since then, and for that reason, millions of lives have been saved. They are not saved by accident or goodwill. Human life is daily deliberately protected from nature by accepted practices of hygiene and medical care, by the control of living conditions and the guidance of human relationships. Mortality statistics are constantly examined to see if the causes of death reveal any areas needing special attention. Because of the success of these practices, the area of public death has, in advanced societies, been taken over by man-made death – once an insignificant or 'merged' part of the spectrum, now almost the whole.

When politicians, in tones of grave wonder, characterize our age as one of vast effort in saving human life, and enormous vigour in destroying it, they seem to feel they are indicating some mysterious paradox of the human spirit. There is no paradox and no mystery. The difference is that one area of public death has been tackled and secured by the forces of reason; the other has not. The pioneers of public health did not change nature, or men, but adjusted the active relationship of men to certain aspects of nature so that the relationship became one of watchful and healthy respect. In doing so they had to contend with and struggle against the suspicious opposition of those who believed that to interfere with nature was sinful, and even that disease and plague were the result of something sinful in the nature of man himself. To this day there survives, amongst some of the well fed and cared for, a nostalgia for the slums of disease.

With this example in mind, the last thing a modern book of the dead should seek is a superstitious or mystical frame of reference. It should avoid the use of faceless generalizations like 'man', 'nature', 'science' and should allow itself only a disciplined use of metaphor. For example, I have introduced the idea of a 'nation of the dead' because this is a readily understandable collective description, but I do not wish to encourage people thereby to sit round in circles discussing The Great Beyond. Nor do I wish to claim mystical authority for the comparison I have made between two kinds of public death – that which results from disease and that which we call man-made. The irreducible virtue of the analogy is that the problem of man-made death, like that of disease, can be tackled only by reason. It contains the same elements as the problem of disease – the need to locate sources of the pest, to devise preventive measures and to maintain systematic vigilance in their execution. But it is a much wider problem and for obvious reasons cannot be dealt with by scientific methods to the same extent as can disease. Indeed the problem of man-made death is so dependent for its solution on clarity of communication that it particularly needs to avoid the pseudo-scientific faults of jargon, of words being used as if they were numbers, and of the dogmatic interpretation of speculative and hypothetical analyses.

Many of these faults so common in modern science already existed in the ancient books of the dead. The *Tibetan Book of the Dead* has an interesting scientific passage on 'the death process':

When the expiration hath ceased, the vital-force will have sunk into the nerve-centre of Wisdom and the Knower will be experiencing the Clear Light of the natural condition. Then, the vital-force being thrown backwards, and flying downwards through the right and left nerves, the Intermediate State momentarily dawns ... The interval between the cessation of the expiration and the cessation of the inspiration is the time during which the vital-force remaineth in the median nerve. The common people call this the state wherein the consciousness-principle hath fainted away.

Although the language of this passage is not much clearer than that of a modern book on social psychology, say, or politics, it is a genuine attempt to analyse a fascinating phenomenon, the moment of death. This is of particular significance to us, if we believe there is no survival after death. For it is in that moment that the value of a person's life and death may be summed up.

The paradox that death the great experience is in fact a non-experience, or the end of experience, mystifies the meaning of the word. When we use it we are probably thinking of a combination of three different stages. There is the period *immediately before* death – 'dying'; the *actual moment*, which novelists describe as 'a sudden void', 'and then nothingness', but which is perhaps an insubstantial line between before and after; and *after-death*, which is the most concrete idea of death because we think of corpses. The 'experience' which fascinates all of us is of course the *actual moment*, the insubstantial line. The passage quoted above from the *Tibetan Book of the Dead* is playing tricks with crossing this line. Once this imaginative leap is made, the idea of

9

death is projected forward into the idea of an afterlife. The *after-death* corpse is a secondary object which will eventually follow the soul – vanguard of the new life – into the afterlife. Death is thus a mystical experience whose active consequences stretch into infinity. But if we do not believe that the line *is* crossed, then the idea of death is projected back, to the period *immediately before* death, and to the life which preceded it. In this case, the significance of death belongs to the general evaluation of life, and the meaning lies specifically in assessments of the value of the individual life and of the manner of dying.

I have said that a modern advanced society cares for the individual life, and has established norms for the time of death and the manner of dying. When someone dies within these norms it is a matter of public concern only in so far as it relates to the degree of progress of medical science. But when someone dies outside these norms it is of the greatest possible public concern. Indeed there is no event of greater moral significance, since the *raison d'être* of *society* is to preserve and enhance life. It is a common confusion, or deception, to talk of the dead as though they were cared for by some gloomy and mystical alliance of God, priests, poets and undertakers, and thus are no concern of the living. In fact, the manner in which people die reflects more than any other fact the value of a society. The details of how and why people die, if traced back to their roots in society, must expose the moral value of living behaviour. And since the manner of dying is a significant definition of 'death', we may say that the values of death, if they can be defined, will have the most important bearing on how society should be conducted.

But how can we discover the values of death? We cannot, as does the *Tibetan Book of the Dead*, invoke special insights into what happens after what 'the common people call ... the consciousness-principle hath fainted away.' But we can evoke the material circumstances of dying: when and how and for what reason; the methods of killing; the condition of the mind and the body in dying.

The materials exist to carry this out in a scientific spirit. However, modern science would not claim to embody the spirit of reason, which is the only sane approach to this subject. In addition to analytical method, we need to retain the human image. The *Egyptian Book of the Dead* does this successfully in its account of the spiritual journey of the soul after death. The soul of the dead man is headed for ethereal glories, but he can still enjoy cakes and ale. His physical parts, including a mouth with the power of magic words, are restored to him in the afterworld. He is rendered, *immune from the bites of serpents and the nibbling of worms . . . Evil spirits are defeated and crocodiles in his path killed . . . He will not be tripped up, or have to eat filth or be boiled in water . . .*

It's delightful. Both the ancient books of the dead are of considerable inspirational value. But I must disencumber the reader of a wrong impression that he might – quite naturally – have formed of the connection between them and the *Twentieth Century Book of the Dead*. When I first proposed this work, under that title, I was startled by some of the expectations it aroused, and by two in particular. One of these was that it would consist of a spiritual charge of a mystical nature – or *psychedelic kick,* to quote the phrase used; the other was that I could not possibly be serious in my intentions. These reactions puzzled me, until it occurred to me that both are based on the assumption that the work would be modelled more or less closely on the ancient books of the dead. I have sought for a way of correcting this misapprehension in a word, and I think I have found the necessary word.

The Egyptian and Tibetan books of the dead are works of *necromancy*. They are concerned with questions such as the raising of the dead, the prescription of right behaviour for the soul after death. They unify life and death by mystifying the distinction between them. In reading them we are offered a temporary liberation from the normal distinctions between external and inner truth.

This book of the twentieth-century dead is, on the contrary, a work of *necrology*. Necrology simply means a naming or listing of the dead. The aim of this work, precisely, is to identify, against a background of knowable fact, the violent dead of the twentieth century in terms of the historical and moral values of a continuing world society. Part of its task is to *de*-mystify. It offers to reconcile life and death only by emphasizing the difference between them.

In seeking to find the correct shape of a twentieth-century book of the dead, the appropriate classes of relationship we should make in composing such a thing, I have become aware of the limitations of this first approach and, inevitably, of the kind of ideal necrological book of the dead which might become possible after thorough and extensive exploration of many aspects on which I have merely touched. That ideal book has become the true model for the present work. Where this one is brief, tentative, elliptic, hypothetical, suggestive, exploratory, that work of the future would be voluminous, expansive, definitional, authoritative, easy in its depth, confident in its relationships. Whether or not I am talking about an actual leatherbound compendium, or whether that is a metaphor for a future area of knowledge, I am convinced the experience of the twentieth century demands that such a book of the dead will come to be written in the human consciousness.

ARE THE DEAD NAMED?

THE famous question, *how many angels can dance on the head of a pin?* is quite sensible, given the basic attempt to externalize symbols and feelings which belong essentially to the mind, the inner life. If that attempt is itself absurd, then so is the question. The same is true of the question, *are the dead named?* If the dead exist in an afterlife, it is sensible to ask, what is the nature of their existence, do they continue to have individual personalities and names, do they eat and drink, may they be tripped up or have to eat filth?

The difference is that the question, *are the dead named?* survives the belief in an afterlife. Even if we don't believe in wise old beardies strumming harps, or halls of glory at the heart of the sun, the question remains meaningful. It slightly changes form, to, do *we* name the dead? It becomes more specific: should we have any attitude at all, should we remember the dead, should we identify and name them? The extreme negative answer, which is that we should concern ourselves only with the living, leads to the proposition that it does not matter how people die, when they are dead we lose interest. It is a view shared by the pseudo-romantic, the brutalized, and the indifferent.

Are the dead named? is one of those questions which assert the very existence of the world of the mind, of those hidden connections between men and between societies which are sometimes but not always and in no guaranteed fashion made externally manifest. If we take the answer for granted, as we do if we value that partly hidden, partly manifest world, then the question becomes, *how* do we name the dead?

The most satisfactory way of naming the dead is the inscription of their names on some commemorative surface such as a tombstone, a plaque, a brass or paper roll or even a newspaper column. The simplest *memento mori* is the best: seeing the name alone we can identify in the most realistic way with human death. In a country churchyard in peaceful times, I can take the names on the tombstones as a sample of the world, and a symbol of my own end. In a similar uncomplex situation, if I look at the names of the military dead, their titles tell me that they died in a special way, which I can comprehend in that same fundamental pattern of relating myself to the world.

But to relate myself to the violent dead of the twentieth century ... when the numbers run into millions ... when the manner of their deaths is so full of the complex and the unknown ... when their identities, not preponderantly military, male, young but a mixture of civilian, female, male, children, military, old, young – when their identities are obscured by the myths of politics, race, class ... How can I relate to this complexity?

In a society such as ours, the complex is taken care of by specialists. Of course! In that case all I need do is call in a qualified mortquean ... A what? A *mortquean*?* What is that? Does it really exist? Well, since in our preoccupation with the really important things in life such as insurance policies, mortgages and the like we tend to be too busy to bother about our relationship with the public dead, we might *deduce* the existence of a

* Pronounced mor'kwin, or if you prefer it, mórt'quean.

class of specialists – call them mortqueans or what you will – who are particularly sensitive and knowledgeable on the subject. Indeed, so trustingly do we invest in the lovely security of missile systems, germ warfare establishments and big bombs that there really *must* be a group of experts somewhere who are anxious to explain to us why we prepare such deaths for ourselves.

Yes, the logic of the situation does postulate the existence of the mortqueans. Hence if they do not exist it may well be necessary to invent them.

Here I confess to a certain puzzlement. It is without doubt that the world is a complex place, and I am content to leave certain aspects of it – the insides of motor cars, varieties of mosses, causes of dental decay, for example – to experts. But the significance of life? Love and sex? My feelings about death? On matters like these I need a direct, simple relationship with the world. I know that learned men are always pointing out how *difficult* and *complex* and *unknown* are such questions. Nevertheless these are not nuts for the learned squirrel, they are as everyday as bread and cheese. However massy becomes the evidence, however tangled and confused the opinions about the public dead, I shall always return to that need for a direct relationship, a simple view of the whole. When we are little we ask the question, Why am I here? and cast around for an adult to answer it. If we persist we discover in time that there is only one adult who can answer it for us, namely our own adult self. It is a pleasant but pernicious habit of learned men, to make us feel like children who only have to ask questions and never answer them. We do have to answer some questions, if we grow up, and answer them for ourselves, and for this reason I shall, for the purposes of this book, resist the invention of the mortquean or expert on death.

It is not that one should avoid the true complexity of events. On the contrary, I have tried to indicate this in Book One, which is a historical survey of the major episodes of organized or large-scale violence, or macro-violence, in the twentieth century. Nevertheless these chapters must be called, as they are, 'sketches', since they attempt with a few strokes of the brush to suggest the human identity of, as well as the patterns of, violence which have created the public dead . . . I can hear these mort-queans groan with the weight of their own sag in the belly of time . . . *O give us flesh and form* . . . *O deliver us* . . . Yes, just let them get at the material and they will supply us with endless correlations and causations and wailings and warnings and theories and theses. Yet much expertise has been expended already on these areas of violence without many serious attempts at *naming the dead*, and I insist that it is this ultimately simple operation on which we are engaged. The reader will appreciate that in naming the dead – so many dead – we shall have to go in for a few complexities of our own. The 'analyses' in Book Two involve the creation of a few new terminologies in order to describe the violent dead of the twentieth century in their different environments. Is it possible that by placing the public dead in context we might arrive at a simple and direct apprehension of their significance? That at any rate is the purpose of these devices. In the final section, Book Three, I attempt to sum up and encapsulate some of the values and meanings that seem to emerge.

Since much of what follows is exploratory and outside of any established discipline, I have based it on a simple statistical framework, the rationale of which is set out in the Statistical Appendix. The primary facts we have, in attempting to name the dead, are numbers of the dead. Much of what is written about violence is based on theories and attitudes extraneous to violence, and I cannot think of anything more lacking and more necessary to the study of violence than a discipline based on the facts of violence. All kinds of intangible notions – such as guilt, brutality, motives, psychological disturbance – are put forward as being the 'facts' of violence, but violence is an event, not a condition. Violence is *always* an event, some say it is the most decisive kind of event possible. Where violence is perpetrated upon human beings, the basic computation of the event is the number of human beings damaged or killed.

The numbers left by the records are seldom accurate, but when we climb into the regions of macro-violence we can at least distinguish between an *order of magnitude* of one million and five million, and achieve a certain perspective of scale. All the figures used in the text are *orders of magnitude*, not definitive or precise figures. Their sources are explained in all cases in the Statistical Appendix. The table on page 215 sets out the basic breakdown as I have calculated it, and in a sense all that follows is a further amplification of that table.

If I have emphasized the need to work through complexity to arrive at a simple relationship between the individual and the public dead, let me suggest that as we work through the complex identities of the violent dead we shall come at every step closer to realizing that what we are dealing with is something indeed very simple and all too easy to relate to: the death of the people in the twentieth century.

Book One

SKETCHES:
PEOPLE IN THE
MACHINES
OF DEATH

2

THE EUROPEAN SOLDIER IN THE FIRST WORLD WAR

Peter in the War Machine

PETER was a shy, wiry lad of nineteen from one of those areas where, as early as 1914 in any large European country, the modern town becomes entangled with the country. He worked in a small factory and lived near fields and woods where he spent hours of his spare time tracking rabbits and potting at wood-pigeons in the tall trees. The trees belonged to the local land-owner but Peter didn't care a fart, one way or the other, about the gentry and would have been considerably embarrassed to be confronted with the local representative of that system. Indeed he was often startled, during army training, by the remote ways of officers as well as the imperative barking and screaming of sergeants. Apart from that he was glad of the chance to see a bit of life and be in with some lads. If life became a bit constricted when they were moved up to farmhouse billets in the rear lines of the Western Front, Peter was not too worried: he kept a quiet corner in the barrack-room. His mate Johnny, a quick city lad, had more the trick of army patter, which is simply that every second word is *fuck* or, for variety, *fucking*.

Some of the older men didn't like the swearing – they were the settled ones that got sentimental over letters from home. Johnny's dirty jokes made him feel equal to those ones, although for the life of him Peter couldn't get his country tongue round those fast four-letter words. Despite his admiration for Johnny, he had the feeling that such language belongs to the gutter.

Peter was better than most with a rifle, and trusted his own skill in the open. He would become a veteran like the few in his platoon who had seen action – that was what he most wanted to happen. Maybe he would meet a girl somewhere after his first action.

A battalion at full strength has about a thousand men. A company has three hundred; this and the platoon are the living centres where relationships and loyalties exist, as in a village. In such a group – like the photographs of the time, a bright aureole of identity blurring into darkness – we find Peter forming up in a line for his first visit to the front. As they march and halt, and march, and halt and march again the group feeling dissolves in the delays and longueurs of divisional movement, the outer darkness of twenty or thirty thousand men presses in on them. When at last they file into trenches to find a stamping-place and a prop for rifles, it is for each man a welcome release of identity from the mass.

How things slip along. What kind of machinery puts a man in the situation where he finds individuality in a hole in the ground, on a bit of wet soil at the level of the rats?

The basic lever was the *conscription law*, which made vast numbers of men available for military service. The civil machinery which ensured the carrying out of this law, and the *military organization* which turned numbers of men into battalions and divisions, were each founded on a bureaucracy. The *production* of resources, in particular guns and ammunition, were a matter for civil organization. The *movement* of men and resources to the front, and the trench system of defence, were military concerns. Civil and military functions were thus meshed – or separated, if you look at it in a different way – at two points: the organizing of numbers, and the mass production and handling of supplies. Behind each of the italicized phrases is a different system, each logical in itself and each capable of being personalized – or rationalized – by those involved. It is reasonable to obey the law, it is good to organize well, it is ingenious to devise guns of high technical capacity, it is sensible to shelter human beings against massive firepower by putting them in protective trenches.

And it is only human to make the best of your surroundings. As the men wait in boredom in the trenches, Peter caresses the knob-end of his rifle bolt with his thumb. He knows every inch of that wood and iron, can feel the clean metal of the bolt and rifling barrel. The order comes to fix bayonets. Others fumble but Peter locks on his bayonet with calm precision. He is complete. Some of them are still swearing as they rattle and fumble with bayonets. The big guns begin to boom, the rising bombardment deafens, shocks them into silence. When it stops there is a long ringing in the ears. No one is able to speak for some time, until Johnny cracks a joke. The others take it up and chatter nervously, the oaths fly about. Each oath is greeted with hysterical laughter by some, others are still and silent. Peter is proud of his mate and his own feelings come back to him. Frankly, he thinks lots of the waiting men don't know what they're in for, are a bit silly almost, don't know how to take care of themselves. The way they swear shows their fear, for they curse their friends, their own commanders and units in the same way as they curse the enemy. Something from the gutter. Peter smiles. He knows who the enemy is, he knows the sights on his rifle are true. He clutches rifle and bayonet into his thigh. A man doesn't need to swear when he is prepared for battle.

Men are climbing over the top. In the scramble – was an order given? – boots dislodge from the trench-wall a flurry of soil that rolls frantically for an instant then lies cold and still in the bottom of the trench. But Peter is running on solid earth, voices are shouting and machine-guns rattling. Shells he never expected are exploding, men seem to disappear into the blast, more are falling than he could ever have imagined. He sees Johnny, in hallucination or real vision, disintegrate, trunk from limbs and head. He seems to hear the explosion that Johnny has vanished into and then the noise and his own scream, 'Fucking bastards!' forced out of him by the blast, for he is part of an explosion himself.

Thus Peter learned the language of the gutter.

Ten million deaths is a cold achievement. There must be – so the story goes – some human motive or emotion, or some over-riding 'cause', that bears a direct relationship to such a reality. Peter's belief that survival depended upon his own skill in a situation, aided by rifle and bayonet, would hardly qualify. We might call this illusion the *fantasy of the bayonet* – in tribute to those millions of citizens who, in field and parade-ground all over the world for fifty years, have been trained to charge roaring at a stuffed dummy. 'Stick it in hard! Shout louder!' – loud enough to drown out the sound of death as you follow-your-bayonet into bullet-hail and shell-blast. (Those who see the bayonet as a sexual symbol are mistaken. It is an extension of the nose.)

However, although it is true that in the First World War deaths came from firepower intensely concentrated in bombardment or mass machine-guns and rifles, and not significantly from bayonets or any other form of personal combat, it was not entirely impersonal. Many of the large battles were made up of concurrent and consecutive series of unit-to-unit engagements. They were personalized – often – in the sense of the battalion or company. Hence the quality of field leadership should make a difference. If a man could identify with his unit could he not be said to be engaged in a personal struggle? What we are looking for here is an organic relationship between Peter and the whole, such as for instance exists in a living society.

Now, in the war of attrition in a concentrated area, where only men and weapons are significant, the strategy (armchair strategists know all this, of course) requires that you offer the bodies of your men to the enemy in large numbers. For it's as important that the enemy should exhaust his firepower as that you should destroy his men. Such a strategy then cancels out any major effects of differentiated leadership in the field. Just as the men of a unit are running about until they are killed or, on a particular occasion, survive; so specific units, if they survive one action, will later be thrown into the pattern of the continuous strategy of attrition. The relationship between Peter and his commanders might then be called the *fantasy of leadership* – in tribute to those feelings of emotion and sympathy between leaders and 'their men' which in some degree existed but which were barely relevant to anything that was happening.

We are left then, so far as organic relationships go, with the 'strategy of attrition'. Strategies are supposed to be the motives of generals. But I don't believe any military expert would claim that the idea of attrition was invented by generals. It was indeed the operating principle of the war almost from the first day to the last, long before the generals thought of pre-empting it as a description of what was happening. The *fantasy of attrition*, alas, is all too near the truth. But it is not, in origin or reality, a human motive. It belongs to the simple logic of the organization of numbers and hardware inherent in the war machine; or, to put it in another way, to the process characteristics of the machine.

The war machine, rooted in law, organization, production, movement, science, technical ingenuity, with its product of six thousand deaths a day over a period of 1,500 days, was the permanent and realistic factor, impervious to fantasy, only slightly altered by human variation. Its function, at first sight, far from being organic, was to destroy every organic thing. Whatever living thing or structure appeared in its path to be destroyed – a man, a tree, a famous regiment, a closely knit platoon, a strategic concept, an illusion of glory – this dull machine rattled on. Whatever diverse threads were shuttled into the operation – a French attack, a plan of sustained bombardment, German use of machine-guns, Russian cavalry charges, four-month or two-week or year-long battles, British generals, new mobile tactics, economic blockade – the same drab fabric of six thousand deaths a day came out the other end.

Yet an organic process of a kind was going on.

On the Western Front, the death-rate of three thousand a day was set in pattern in the first months of the war, in the massive confrontation of the armies along the 300-mile frontiers from Switzerland to the North Sea. So powerful was the fantasy of the bayonet that the French in their numerous battles of 1914 charged in mass formation into the German machine-guns and shells, to be mown down and charge again to be mown down and charge. In two months half a million men died, ten thousand a day, and by the end of the year after the last-ditch battle of the Marne near Paris and the smaller British involvement at Ypres, the total was brought to near a million deaths. So that the death-rate did not grow, or 'escalate' in the later years: the pattern was made and merely repeated itself in different settings.

How the fantasy of leadership must have grown as men and their leaders settled into the trenches of 1915 to face the constant repetitions of death, at Neuve-Chapelle, Artois, Loos, 2nd Ypres – already the place-names begin to recur. Many of the set-piece battles were fought in an area no larger than four or five miles square, with fields, woods, villages, perhaps a river. About the area of a small or large town, depending on the numbers engaged. Ten days of battle – a fair minimum, given that you bombard the enemy for a couple of days to destroy and demoral-ize him, then send your troops at him in numbers; then he, undestroyed and undemoralized, pushes you back and bombards you; all this before you can think of stopping – will bring ten times four thousand deaths. Armchair strategists will confirm these figures. It may be considerably more than forty thousand deaths, or a bit less, but a certain minimum is guaranteed by the mere presence of numbers and massive firepower aimed directly at them.

And now the fantasy of attrition – the delusion of the generals that this process was somehow controlled by them to the extent of being called a 'strategy' – brings us to the year 1916 and the simple logic of that year. The larger the numbers engaged, the longer the battle is likely to last. So if kept up for one month you will have a hundred and twenty thousand deaths, enough to populate your large town if this was an area of the living not the dead. It takes four months, by this logic, to create a real city of the dead, half a million dead in a desert pitted with shell-holes. A city like the Somme, half a million dead in four months. And Verdun, a vast metropolis of death that straggles on past its four months and its half million into the smoky suburbs of a year-long attrition and one million dead.

In 1917, as the names of the towns and cities of the dead roll, rattle and boom – Arras, Chemin-des-Dames, Messines, Passchendaele, Cambrai, 3rd Ypres – we can begin to see some-thing of the organic process that is going on. For now the politi-cians decide that there will be no negotiated peace, we will create more brave deaths in order to achieve total surrender, we will starve the Germans into submission. Beyond mere illusion, policy is now firmly based on corpses. Out of the destructive process of the machine, and men's adaptation to it, something quite substantial has been created: an organism in society which feeds on death, which aggrandizes itself on numbers of the dead. By 1918, when the military machine is recovering its mobility and passing towards a conclusion over the old scenes of death – Arras, Chemin-des-Dames, 2nd Marne, Amiens, Arras and Verdun, Cambrai, Saint-Quentin – the larger war machine has gripped Germany in economic blockade and a million civilians starve to death.

Post-mortem, the morbidity of the social organism persists. The binding emotions of war hysteria, pride, patriotism, tomato-ketchup heroism, allied to the machine to give to death the qualities of a negative organism, now turn to recrimination and self-justification. The fighting quality of men, the quality of field leadership, the mistakes of generals, are 'blamed'. The more sophisticated hunt their witches amongst the 'war-mongers', the war profiteers, the arms manufacturers and other conspirators. The historians begin a search for the 'causes' of the war. The 'causes' magnify in monstrous proportion to the magnitude of the event. When discovered, the monsters are to be strangled and that will be the end of war. But the most subtle morbidity, the most heartbreaking mixture of perception and unawareness, is that of the military intellectuals. They know that the catastrophe is rooted in scale and quantity, in the size of the war machine and its technical failures. So they will reform the war machine, recapture military mobility, streamline its mechanisms, root it more firmly and efficiently in the industrial base, make it more successful. It does not occur to them that the spreading destructiveness of the war machine is due to its success, not its failure.

The one thing that stands out over all is that at no time, before, during or after the war, was there a living organic structure in society with sufficient strength to resist the new man-made and machine-made creation: organic death.

3

THE RUSSIANS IN THE
TWENTIETH CENTURY

THE CIVIL WAR PERIOD, 1917-21

Pavel in the Death-Breeding Machine

IN the early spring of 1918, Pavel saw the deaths of his mother
and his little sister. He had been playing on his own, half a mile
outside the village, when a party of soldiers clattered by. Pavel
raced to catch up with them. His lungs were bursting with
excitement. The din and bustle of the horses surged in his blood
even after they had passed out of hearing. By the time he
reached the edge of the village the little wooden houses were so
quiet he thought they must have galloped straight through. Then
he heard the neighing of horses, he saw a soldier come out of a
neighbour's house carrying something wrapped in a blanket.
Familiar village voices were raised in protest. Pavel approached
the backyard of his own house cautiously. His father was
fighting in the Russian Army, and he knew the Germans were
the enemy. He crouched down by a tree a few yards from the
door of his house. Unfamiliar noises came from inside. A
succession of moans, shrieks, whimpers was eventually replaced
by a monotonous howling.

Incredibly, the door of the house opened. Two soldiers came
out. His little sister was clinging to the leg of one of them, she
began to scream in a tantrum as the soldier tried to shake her off.
Pavel wanted to shout at her to stop being a nuisance. Her
screams made him boil with annoyance. He had an urge to rush
forward and give her a good clip on the side of the head,
to show that he could control her. Then a strange thing happened. As if to express Pavel's irritation, the soldier bent
down and in one swift movement tore the little girl from his

side, hauled her up in the air and threw her against the side of the house.

The soldiers walked on. After a few paces they stopped, turned round and stared at the little girl's body, lying still on the ground. One shouted something at the other which Pavel could not quite understand, then they walked off talking loudly.

The actions of the soldiers in these few seconds had impressed Pavel in a curious way, so that when he finally left his hiding place and approached the body of his sister, it was almost with calm and detachment. She looked ugly and dead. He was surprised to find that the blood from the wound on her head had congealed there and dried on the side of her face. He went into the house. Little was disturbed. All the familiar objects were in place. Only, his mother lay on the bed in fantastic disarray. The bedclothes were rumpled and dirty, her dress was torn, her legs were in some queer kind of mess. Her face was half covered by a pillow. The sight of his mother, usually so primly tidy, in this state, and the knowledge that she must have been responsible for the unearthly howling, revolted him. Pavel approached the head of the bed and tried to lift the pillow. She was gripping it tightly with one hand and resisted his tug. In a sudden rage he tore it from her. He hated the look in her revealed eyes. With hate and rage for his mother he realized that she was dead.

He stood with the pillow in his hand. For a long time his eyes dully took in the same details with no apparent effect. Then the hate for his mother would return. But that, and everything else he felt, was strange and new. It was as if all his senses rubbed along the sharp edge of a scythe to the point where he passed over into numbness again. The scene of the soldiers kept recurring. It was the ease with which the soldier had thrown his sister against the wall that impressed him. Then they had walked on, stopped and turned. One said something – a word of congratulation? – to the other. Then they walked off briskly chatting. Pavel tried to catch the sense of this novel, easy kind of power the soldiers seemed to have. The scene faded from his mind, the hate for his mother returned, the scythe in his head unbearably shrilled, numbness took over. Then the soldiers again.

At last Pavel was jerked out of the rut by a new fact which had gradually seeped into his mind. The soldiers had spoken in Russian! He dropped the pillow and moved toward the door. If the soldiers were Russian he must catch up with them. He became obsessed with this one fact. They might help him to find his father, who was also a Russian soldier. He took the road out of the village in an odd turmoil of notions. He had wanted to leave his mother and sister for some time, and join his father fighting the Germans. And then, if these soldiers were not Germans, were they the enemy because they had killed his mother and sister? Who was the enemy, and why had Russians made him hate his mother and almost forget that his little sister had ever existed? By nightfall the twelve-year-old Pavel was wandering far from what had, only that morning, been his family home.

In the West, our view of the Russian Civil War has been conditioned by its connection with the First World War and Allied Intervention; by the exploits of specific White Armies – Deniken, Wrangel, Kolchak: on the other side, by the shaping directives of Lenin and the growth of the Red Army; the growth of the Cheka and the Red Terror; the part played by the Social Revolutionaries and Anarchists. In short, by the influences of diplomatic history and the documentation of the early Communist state.

Given these bold lines of significance, the actual substance of the Civil War period has tended to be seen as a background of confusion. We look at the basic phenomenon of disorder – the break-up of the Russian Empire through the world war and Revolution, the consequent administrative collapse, the revolts in the Baltic States and Poland and the troubles three thousand miles away in Siberia, the upheavals in the Ukraine and further south – and we call this a confusion of vastness. We look at the ten million who died and we call this a confusion of the unknown.

Nevertheless the substantial experience of the period was hardship and death among the civilian population at large, and in these terms no written history exists. My sketch for a substantial history of the Civil War period in Russia would begin with a shape something like a pyramid:

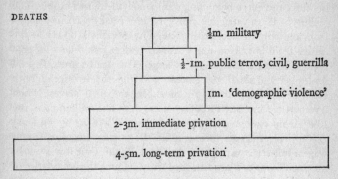

DEATHS

½m. military

½-1m. public terror, civil, guerrilla

1m. 'demographic violence'

2-3m. immediate privation

4-5m. long-term privation

HARD VIOLENCE: Estimate 2-3 million deaths

PRIVATION: Estimate 6-8 million deaths

This is really a very important shape. You could say it was the shape of violence in the twentieth century. However, before rushing to such grandiose conclusions let me mention a few of its specific significances. Very roughly, in its proportion of hard violence to privation deaths, it would express most of the major civil wars of the century. More finely, in the actual types of death noted and in the magnitude of the whole, it is similar to the pattern of civilian deaths in the Second World War in Russia and China. But its most striking significance in the history of violence is its chronological position. The foundations of massive military attrition were laid in the First World War. The foundations of massive civilian attrition were laid immediately afterwards, and on precisely the same scale. Some notes on the nature of the different types of violence involved in this particular attrition will indicate how the scale, in each case, is achieved.

Hard Violence

Top tier: Half a million military deaths. The armies opposing the Reds were small – between five thousand and thirty thousand in strength – such as would not normally be a danger to any well-organized state. That they were able to threaten the centre of power was due to the fact that the Red Army was built from nothing, and in the beginning was a small, ill-trained rabble. The feeling of heroic struggle conveyed in Trotsky's *History* stems from the particular crisis of defending Bolshevik power at the centre from attack on many fronts. It does not reflect an epic feeling amongst the people at large. The deaths arose from a multiplicity of small engagements and from the practice on both sides of shooting their prisoners. In the final stages, when Trotsky had increased military strength to five million men, the Red Army was able to sweep the last White Army into the Black Sea, crush its former allies the peasant anarchists, and wage a full-scale war against the Poles. By this time it was not so much civil war as a large modern army defining the boundaries of a new empire.

Second tier: Public terrorism; civil violence and guerrilla activities: half a million to one million deaths.

Public terrorism. Most of us have a simple image of post-revolutionary violence, derived from the French Revolution: the people rise up and kill the masters, then the new regime takes over and institutes a bloody terror. However, the French *aristos* were numerically a tiny minority, easily identifiable in a personal, individual sense. The Russian bourgeoisie, several million strong and representing the fabric of organized social life – administration, the professions, business, law, church – could be identified only as an abstract *class*. They could not be led in convenient batches to the guillotine. What were the actual points of contact in the killing of bourgeois, and on what scale did it take place? Some of the party leaders, in their fear after a murder attempt on Lenin, proclaimed a policy of terror against counter-revolutionaries and bourgeois. The injunction was taken up chiefly by the secret police. Seeking out, imprisoning and executing 'enemies of the revolution', that is members of the bourgeoisie to a large extent arbitrarily and indiscriminately selected, became the means of growth of the Cheka as an influence-seeking organization. This was the heart of the 'Red

Terror'. An estimate of 50,000 victims in the Civil War period has been considered too low; but the number could hardly have exceeded 100,000 given the size of the Cheka and their range of operations at that time.

Members of the armed forces, particularly sailors, also to some extent took the injunction to heart. That is to say, individuals acting unofficially but wearing the uniform of the regime committed arbitrary acts against other individuals wearing the appearance of the bourgeoisie. There was also a counter-terror from the soldiers of the White Armies. Stories of atrocities, 'mass executions' and individual acts of violence were numerous. However, sailors are confined to ports; the numbers and scale of operations of Red and White Armies were very limited. In these conditions it takes a tremendous number of violent incidents, and even of 'mass killings', which in such circumstances usually means about five to twenty people (though there would be a few on a larger scale), to accumulate to a total of, say, 50,000 deaths.

Acts of terror, then, by the Cheka and the armed forces accounted for something between 100,000 and 200,000 deaths. I have called this kind of violence 'public terror' in order to convey its semi-official character. In theory both the Cheka and the military were subject to government direction and discipline; in practice the Cheka, and those members of the armed forces disposed to extra-curricular violence, tended to define the limits of their own authority.

Civil violence and guerrilla activities. In reading about the confusions and turmoils of any civil war it is easy to form the impression that everyone is going about shooting everyone else. It doesn't happen. Hard violence at the man-to-man level is always in some degree selective. The most intensive unofficial violence seems to have occurred in the southern parts of Russia from the Ukraine to the Urals. In these areas, where authority was disputed, numerous bands of peasant guerrillas warred with one another and against regular forces. In some regions terrorist groups sought out and persecuted landlords and Jews. Criminal gangs also terrorized some areas. It seems likely the total numbers engaged in such activities would be at the level of 50/100,000. It is possible to imagine much larger numbers engaged at different times in brief and ineffectual revolts – 'risings of the people'. But so soon as men engage in killing activities for any sustained length of time they are identifiable as minority groups in terms of their motivation – politics, physical displacement from home, personal tendencies to violence – and of their organization – the supply of arms and food over a period. Assuming such activities to be more widespread than those of the terror, but less effectively violent than the military operations, we might calculate the deaths brought about by such means in the region of 300,000.

The total for public terror, civil violence and guerrilla activities would then be about half a million deaths. Allowing for a serious underestimate in these calculations, particularly in the more unofficial kinds of violence occurring over the country as a whole, a figure of half a million to one million deaths would keep the matter in perspective.

Third tier: Demographic violence. One million deaths. This figure is conjectural, and so is the concept of 'demographic violence'. It means a kind of violence which, for a time, is as habitual amongst a massive section of the people as, say, the habit of buying bread.

In the reporting of social phenomena there is a permanent distinction to be noted between journalism and, for example, sociology. The journalist often reports the striking and unusual event, the sociologist looks for the norm. A journalist reports that some people suffered from food poisoning after eating bread. A sociologist tells us that one out of every ten people in the population buys bread every day. In the one case the event itself is important; in the other, it is the measurement of an unremarkable event that is significant. Since periods of violence are by nature 'unusual and striking' we are much dependent upon the journalist for our primary information. All the more so because large-scale violence does not operate within known norms: it tends to create its own norms.

The killings of the public terror, mentioned above, were much reported to the world and are given prime place in histories of the period. Yet such events are part of the collective experience of a society only in so far as it reads the newspapers, absorbs information, discusses rumour. What we must ask is, was there any kind of violence which was part of the total collective experience in actuality? In estimating deaths from unofficial civil violence, I have left a margin of half a million. This is because it is not clear to me how far such violence in fact penetrated to the roots of communal life, that is, was demographic in character. Again, the histories are full of stories of robber gangs, of displaced bands of violent men, wandering the countryside. Over a period of four years such violence has time to penetrate. Nevertheless, it is my impression that, whilst it would create a general climate of disorder and insecurity, such violence would produce, in terms of actual deaths, something closer to the lower than the higher estimate.

The roots of communal life, in Russia, were the villages. In reality, several hundred thousand villages where life centred, not on the public events emanating from the cities, but on local traditions and relationships. Any reports of the events of revolution, civil war, disorder penetrating to 'every village' are thus likely to contain considerable exaggeration. However, economic events did penetrate. Money values had fallen drastically. The grain market had broken down. Peasants were therefore storing their grain instead of taking it to market. In the summer of 1918 the Bolshevik government decreed forcible grain requisitions in the areas it undisputedly held, chiefly north and central Russia. About a hundred detachments of workers, each with about a hundred men, and with machine guns, went out to enforce the requisitions where necessary. There was great resistance from the peasants, and a degree of bloodshed. But this still does not come anywhere near 'every village'. However, *in every village* Poor Peasants Committees were set up to supervise grain requisitions, and distribution of agricultural equipment and other matters. The unintended result was the 'bread war' of June–November 1918.

I have not seen an estimate of deaths in the bread war except in collective terms. There was enormous violence. Men were hanged, beaten and burned to death. The Committees had to be disbanded because of the violence. It was a 'war'.

Suppose we translate all this into measured terms. The rural population under Bolshevik authority at the time was roughly fifty million. In a notional distribution of one hundred thousand villages each containing five hundred people, in each of which the cumulative deaths over a period of six months' intensive violence might easily reach a total of ten, the accumulated number of deaths would be one million. In micro-terms, in the village authority was suddenly given to people who were not remotely experienced in its use. They were given power to take possessions from their richer fellows, who had been accounted, and would still feel, superior to them and who may have ill-used them in the past. It is not the sort of arrangement to which any agricultural community, anywhere in the world, would respond with smooth compliance. It is not necessary to postulate the so-called backwardness of the Russian peasant in order to imagine the resentments, the tensions, the paying-off of old scores, the first beatings, the first deaths and the further violence that inevitably follows. Moreover, whatever the exact distribution, whether or not the bread war occurred in literally 'every village', it seems almost certainly an example of like-minded behaviour on a massive scale. Five or ten or more deaths might be 'absorbed' in the lives of almost every village as a phenomenon of disorder, without being so journalistically striking as public terror in the cities. It is more what the sociologists call 'mass behaviour'. For six months the peasants were, as you might say, buying bread with a vengeance.

Privation
Fourth tier: Immediate privation, 2–3 million.
Bottom tier: Long-term privation, 4–5 million.
Total: 6–8 million deaths.

Consider the death-breeding machine, which generates death as from a vacuum.

Several million men have already died in three years of the world war. The army has virtually disintegrated in the field. The new regime has signed a peace treaty. At home, in the towns and cities, industry has run down. Inflation is destroying the market in goods. Supplies to heat and light people's homes are reducing. Sanitation and other town services are failing. Transport to carry food from the villages, and the grain market itself, are breaking down. That is the economic vacuum, in the summer of 1918.

People, in their need for food, rush in to fill the vacuum. Tens of thousands travel between the towns and villages. Some stay there, to be close to the source of food. Others bring back food to the towns. In the villages, a barter system develops; in the towns, a black market in food. Those who cannot travel, or survive black market negotiations, are starving to death.

Towards the end of summer, a worldwide epidemic of lethal influenza reaches Russia. It spreads rapidly in the cities. The popular food traffic carries it into the villages. In the cities, the proportion of flu victims who die is heightened by the old poverty, the new hunger, and overcrowded living conditions. The flu does its damage in a matter of weeks. It is succeeded by a series of typhus epidemics. Sanitation services have now broken down completely in the towns. Typhus is able to spread widely, and over a longer period. As winter comes on, heating and lighting services have also collapsed. There is to be no warmth, and no light.

But what of the people who are supposed to keep things going? The bourgeois industrialists, managers, administrators, businessmen, the well-off peasants or kulaks. These are the people whose working lives are sensitive to the economic machine. In terms of immediate survival, they represent the essential social fabric. Some of the bourgeois have fled or joined White Armies or are seeking food for themselves; others are uncertain of their position, of what to produce, what to organize, to whom to give orders, from whom to receive them. The kulaks are uncertain of their markets. This is the social vacuum.

The Bolsheviks are no more than another element in the death-breeding machine. Their immediate concern is with their own political survival. This they are fighting out on the military fronts and in numerous struggles in outlying parts of the empire. They have no political relationships with the spectrum of classes, interests and people at large in the sense that a government must have if it is to govern. Their answer to the social vacuum is to provoke hostility and terror against the bourgeois. Their answer to the economic vacuum is to 'blame' the kulaks for the shortage of food, accuse them of hoarding grain, send armed detachments amongst them and set up the disastrous Poor Peasants Committees. In truth, their solutions are based on long-term theories of class which have no relevance, or have counter-relevance, to the immediate situation. Perhaps it is instinctive and inevitable that such a regime, with only long-term visions, should project responsibility for the immediate situation on to a particular section of society. At any rate, between the immediate situation of the Bolsheviks, and that of the people, there is no connection. That is the political vacuum.

By the end of the winter of 1918/19, in the towns and cities under Bolshevik rule with a population of ten to fifteen million, perhaps one person in every five, or two to three million, has died: from hunger, epidemic influenza and typhus, and the effects of a Russian winter on dark, unheated homes.

I have called this 'immediate privation', the first massive blow of the death-breeding process against the civilian population at large. In the longer term, over the years, 1919, 1920, 1921, the wasting attrition continues. The peasants, in reaction to the enforced grain collections and the hostile attitude of the regime, have reduced the areas sown with grain by one half, so that the total supply of food throughout the country to those who do not produce it has been reduced to near starvation level. Perhaps a million or more people die in each of those years – about the same rate as deaths on the Western Front – throughout Russia from the effects of privation. By 1921 the regime has issued ration cards for bread to large sections of the population. Workers receive four times as much as bourgeois. The regime is in control of things to that extent: it has given a particular shape to death.

And Pavel? Old Pavel, wanderer, expert in death, camp follower: what became of that ancient lad? At fifteen, hard, brown, and rather dirty, quick and shrewd, with the dead eyes inherited from his mother, Pavel had never killed, although . . . stripping corpses, bartering clothes, gold teeth, ammunition for food . . . the armies loosened up the terrain wonderfully for boys in this business. Only once was Pavel ever in the big city, and even he was appalled by what he found there. Never able to get away from dying, this Huckleberry Finn of the steppes. Back to the armies and the bodies. But this time Pavel was quick to sense that the retreating White Army, with a growing number of refugees in its train, was no longer a survivor's bet. He was pushed right back to the old game of thieving in the villages, lifting eggs in a peasant's backyard, something he hadn't done since he was twelve or thirteen ...

At first he thought the flurry of noise was ... indignant chickens, of course ... but no, an angry human, large as ... waving a stick. He needed those eggs, Pavel, they were his passport to employment with the Red Army detachment that had just moved into the village. The peasant was too angry to protect himself. Pavel picked up a stone, quickly. The man's head jerked back as the rock hit him full in the face. He fell. In seconds Pavel stripped off the peasant smock, his technical instinct diagnosing death as he did so. He was able to pack in nearly a dozen eggs before rising panic made him gather up the improvised sack and run.

Reaching a corner, he slowed down his pace to a prudent walk. Turning the corner, his heart counterleapt in his slowed-down body. A party of soldiers was marching towards him. A voice shouted, 'That's one of them!' Some villagers were standing about. Pavel tried to locate the voice. But the soldiers had stopped. A hand grasped his shoulder. Before he could protest, he was roughly shoved in with four or five other civilians around whom the soldiers formed a stiff enclosure.

The marching cell continued along the street with Pavel now one of its prisoners. He tried grinning at the soldiers but they stared straight ahead. They were unlike the ones he had known. He smiled thinking of the eggs. They would see him through when they reached headquarters. But why had he been denounced? He was unknown in this village. Was an enemy merely someone who was unfamiliar?

Inside a minute he had stopped thinking of such things. They were not going to any headquarters, but moving out of the village. And there were four other prisoners, to be exact. Pavel addressed the sergeant up ahead, loudly, explaining his position. The sergeant ignored him. He tried again, but now each time he spoke the other prisoners joined in with their protests. The soldiers marched on. Pavel relaxed. He spotted the field they would use before the sergeant gave the order to halt. He watched the others become aware of what was happening as they were filed along the edge of a wood. By the time the five civilians were lined up facing the soldiers, Pavel was the only silent one amongst them.

SOCIAL WAR, 1930-50

Katya in the Total State Machine

LENIN once said that the essential question in politics is 'Who – whom?' There are a number of suitable ways of completing the syntax of that blunt phrase, such as *dominates, fools, sleeps with, bribes, co-operates with, kills, votes for,* and so forth. However, leaving aside violent assumptions of the 'essential' type of activity, politics is certainly a question of relationships and identities, and this the formula 'who-whom?' neatly expresses.

Any politician in his right mind recognizes that the methods he uses in his political relationships must be conditioned by the nature and size of the group he is dealing with. At the bluntest level of persuasion, he may imprison or kill one of his political rivals. The same personal methods might do for a large but cohesive group; in so far as it reacts as one, the suppression of a few might persuade the rest that they know when they're beaten; although our (rather vicious) politician would also have to resort to subtler pressures to break the power of such a group. At any rate, when dealing with the people at large, or any of its major classes, the most vicious he can get (whilst remaining in his right mind) is to impose severe economic and legal pressures, because the people at large do not react as one and he can have no personal relationship with them.

Now, the specific identities of such groups change with time and circumstance. The top political people may be nobles,

Bolsheviks, friends of the President, cabinet and shadow cabinet. Cohesive groups: trade unions, the nobility, the Bolshevik party, upper bourgeoisie, women-for-Nixon, the clergy, and so forth. Even the people at large change their identities: workers, serfs, bourgeois, women voters, peasants, technicians. But the broad quantitative divisions remain constant. The most ingenious theorizing can't alter the fact that every society has a vast number of people; that the top decisions are taken by a collection of people who by and large know one another; and that in between there are cohesive groups with solid political identity. That is to say, there is a classically constant rationale that quantitatively conditions the kinds of who-whom relationships feasible in politics. The politician that tried to dispose of a rival by subjecting him to severe fiscal pressure would be out of his head; it would be equally absurd to try to imprison or kill the people at large.

With that piece of commonsense firmly tucked under our backsides we can now examine the event mythically known as the 'liquidation of the kulaks'. 'The liquidation of the kulaks as a class', in line with Marxist doctrine, was advocated by the Bolshevik ideologists: that is, severe economic measures, including expropriation, against the rich peasants in order to destroy their influence. Stalin had already used his *opposition* to this policy as an excuse to purge the Left of the party: that is, to imprison or kill his rivals. In 1929 however, the Stalin group decided on rapid collectivization: a hundred million peasants were to be forced into collective farms over a short space of time. 'Liquidation of the kulaks as a class' became official policy, as a cover for the actual sequence of events. As in the Civil War, workers' detachments and Poor Peasants Committees were to enforce compliance in the villages, with the help of the secret police. Millions of peasants, not only kulaks, resisted. After a period of violence reminiscent of the bread war of 1918, lasting about six months, a halt was called because of the extent of the killing. Responsibility for the bloodshed was projected on to the executors of the party's orders.

In 1931 the massive and final collectivization drive was launched. The workers and Poor Peasants Committees had not been enthusiastic in destroying their fellows, and the drive was now firmly in the hands of the secret police. Killing of resisters was resumed in more orderly fashion. In 1932 a degree of drought reduced harvest levels. Nevertheless the secret police and party operatives continued ruthless collections of grain from peasant holdings. A man-made famine ensued, in which millions starved. In these and succeeding years, massive deportations of peasants took place, to 'settlements' and labour camps in Siberia.

Ten million peasants died. Five million in the man-made famine. Probably two million in the machine-gun violence, the executions and the immediate hardship of being ejected from their homes. And three million in the labour camps.

These events brought completely new dimensions into the logic of internal state violence. The types of violence used, apart from the deportations, were similar to those used in the Civil War. Even the proportional relationship between hard violence and privation was about the same. So that the events themselves, to many who took part, were like a recrudescence of the Civil War. But their evolutionary effects created something quite new: the death machine of the total state, on the scale at which it operated from that time forward until the death of Stalin.

The who-whom relationship between the politician – the Leader – and the people at large was now not on the basis of economic pressures or political persuasion, but on the imprison-or-kill basis. The technologies of violence had aggrandized sufficiently during the collectivization to make this possible. Although some of the technologies were imitative of those accidentally evolved during the Civil War, they were now directed by a new consciousness of purpose embodied in the people who ran them: the aggrandized secret police.

The who-whom relationship was thus on the same basis for the three classic quantitative groups: the politician's personal rivals, the cohesive political group (including the secret police itself when necessary), and the people at large, all were to be terrorized into submission by the imprison-or-kill method.

But what of the identity of those on the *whom* end of this bargain? They could not officially be called 'victims of terror' or 'those who were killed for opposing'. The answer was evolved in the collectivization by the use of the fantasy-phrase 'liquidation of the kulaks as a class'. They were not a 'class', they were ten million people. They were not 'kulaks', they were peasants including some kulaks. They were not 'liquidated', they were shot, starved and imprisoned to die. But the myth provided a lead. Future victims would be assigned an identity – such as spy, wrecker, saboteur, deviationist – which bore no relation to themselves but would serve the purpose of mythifying the acts of imprisoning and killing. I have made up the word *paranthropoid* to describe this form of identity, because it goes beyond the human identity of the person, beyond his political or economic identity, beyond the human actions which identify his arrest, imprisonment and death: beyond all these, into unreality. The person is treated in a way to which he cannot intelligibly respond as a human being, or even as a political or economic animal; he cannot respond at all; he is a paranthropoid. This completes the who-whom relationship of Stalinism.

As to the psychology of the paranthropist, we can go into that later; but it is a mistake to assume the cold brutal or the cold ideological stereotype. Many Western writers have promoted the feeble legend that those ten million people were destroyed 'because' they were 'backward peasants' holding back the progress of Russian industrialization. Yet to resist eviction from your home at gunpoint is not a manifestation of backwardness, and it has nothing to do with being a peasant. The ways of paranthropy are many.

There is one more aspect of the evolution of violence to which the collectivization may be relevant. Many analyses exist of early manifestations of the Bolsheviks – the ideological fanaticism, the growth of the Cheka, the personal character and paranoia of Stalin – suggesting that these led 'inevitably' to the mass terror; that is that the qualitative characteristics led inevitably to the quantitative reality. At any rate, there is a sense in which it was the *quantitative* reality, as evolved in the escalating violence of the collectivization, that led to the qualitative effects – the weird logics and distortions – that we see as the hallmarks of totalitarianism.

Those theorists who advocate political violence would do well to develop their logic in terms of quantitative realities. They ... putter about, don't they, with their genteel euphemisms ... liberation liquidation ... ideology class purity ... nervously waving their hands before their tense cassocks like bishops in a brothel. I eagerly await publication of a General Theory of Violence which asserts that an industrializing state needs a reserve pool of prisoners, with near a million of them dying every year, just so that the state bosses can have elbow room to exercise their authority ... as some economists still argue that the capitalist state should have a vast pool of unemployed, so that the bosses can always be 'right', need never adapt to new conditions or take radically new decisions. That at any rate was the logic of terror, of the total-state machine under Stalin.

Who is Katya? Or, since it's an upside-down world, *whom* is Katya? – in terms of objective reality, that is. Watch her put on her clothes. Not hurriedly, although she's been wakened up in the middle of the night ... not drowsily, although her face is still white with sleep ... Katya is concentrating, despite those wisps of hair ... She doesn't seem to care about how she looks. Is that natural in a woman? And the way she seems to be thinking about something ... Not so innocent as she looks, that's obvious. Oh ... the clothes ... just look, skirt, blouse and stockings. O subtle! Could anything more cunningly disguise the identity of a ... saboteur? foreign spy? ... than that simple grey blouse, dark skirt, long woollen stockings. Reactionary element? Wrecker? Never mind, they'll sort that out once they get you there. It'll be on the files. Get your coat on. By the way ... why the woollen stockings? Do you think ...

In the prison. It's a matter of time, now, isn't it. Or timelessness. Even time is objective now, enclosed in space. Stone walls ... (do not a prison make. Oh no? Well, we'll concede that much to objective reality. Stone walls do make a prison.) Katya sneezes. Katya wants to go to the lavatory. Come on, leave off those intimate details. Who is she? Perhaps her husband has already gone the same way; is that why ... But the state does not pry into such matters, your grief's your own, if that's what it is. And you still have your name. Privacy. Time. Days. They tell Katya her sentence, she's got five years. What do you mean, when's the trial? Oh, there's been a mix-up. Let's see, yes, the trial is fixed for next Tuesday. Well, now you know the sentence you won't be apprehensive about it. Those filing-systems! There you are, Katya, you've had a glimpse into the great world of objectivity. And you still have your name. You can hug your name to yourself on the train journey. Katya.

But who is she? Pity we didn't get a look at the file. Collaborator? Enemy of socialism? A genuine paranthropoid, anyway. You wouldn't know from the expression on her face. Take that irrelevant look off your face, Katya. Don't tell me you *enjoy* sitting on the floor of a rolling goods waggon for two weeks ... You ought to look brave, or resentful: one of the two. Stop making a mystery of yourself. You talked to all those others in the prison, didn't you ... quite pleasantly, as if you'd all expected to find one another there. And you keep giving food to that frightened boy in the waggon. Why don't you ... Look here, you'll have to wake your ideas up a bit. Don't imagine you'll get off lightly with your five years. Do you think they'll let a dangerous element like you back into society? They'll re-sentence you, if you last that long, and that's not likely. And what's more, you won't be needing that name once the train stops, they'll give you a number ...

Perhaps she's one of those backward peasants. Let's see, what year are we in? About three million peasants to the labour camps around 1930, then in the next five or six years they took out about two million other types. They mopped up a lot of rotten bourgeois elements in those years – businessmen, technicians, priests and other religious people – as well as workers who were wrecking the economy, and of course those bolshie types that always say the wrong thing. Nineteen-thirty-six and thirty-seven were the great years, of course. A million shot in the prisons and another five million off to the camps. Just like the Civil War or the collectivization all over again. That must have been a time of great nostalgia for the secret police. Katya might easily have been one of that lot. Real enemies of the people, they were, I mean six million people can't be right, can they? They kept the levels well up after that, what with the war ... saboteur elements, Polish prisoners, German prisoners of war, Russian soldiers captured by the Germans because they were too cowardly to die ... collaborators after the war, and then the big purge of '48/49 ... who knows, maybe another five million. We're only counting the ones that died, of course, perhaps fifteen million all told. They let a lot out after Stalin died ...

So what's so special about your train, Katya? It stops, like all the rest, fifty degrees colder than where it started from. That nervous boy gave up, did he? Well, some aren't tough enough even to get there, they just die in the waggon. That's life – objectively speaking, of course. There's a hut for Katya, with fifty others, and a number, and twelve hours' work a day. Not much point in describing the surroundings. There aren't any, apart from ice and snow on the ground and meaningless forests. Katya works hauling timber. What, you mean they make Katya, a woman... No, no you've got it wrong. Look, there's this piece of timber. It looks pretty enormous but if you put twenty people at one end ... it doesn't matter if they're in rags, it's a scientific fact that there's enough motive power there to lift one end up ... even if four or five of them only have a few weeks left in them. And what difference does it make whether that lousy little saboteur is at one end of the log or the other ? You've got to look at it objectively. Anyway, you can see from the filthy condition she's in that she has a thoroughly criminal mind ... Well, that's after six months, when Katya has a permanent stiffness in her joints and an anal haemorrhage is making it difficult for her to ...

Just a minute, this is going beyond the bounds of decency, we don't need filthy talk of this kind ... Anyway, what about the real Katya, we never heard about that? Where's the human interest, the sympathy, the suffering ... You don't expect us to relate to this ... subhuman creature ... paranthropoid ...?

Who?

Actually, the labour camps weren't all that bad. The death-rate in many of them probably wasn't more than five per cent every year; or, if you count the high proportion of every new intake that failed to make the initial survival adjustment and died within the first year ... maybe between five and eight per cent. That's not much worse than the death-rate in the Polish ghettoes under the Nazis, in some cases even better. And that rate would have been considerably lowered if it hadn't been so cold. After all, there must be lots of people that can't stand up very long to temperatures of sixty below zero. If it had been possible to provide them with proper clothing against such iron temperatures, and body sustenance in the form of nourishing food, and cut down the work ratios and give them a couple of days off a week, then the whole business would be right in line with objective reality ... healthy socialist correction, contribution of labour camps to the national economy. So it could have been not too bad. Admittedly there were some camp regions that sustained a death-rate approaching thirty per cent every year. That's pretty awful. Thirty per cent must be about the maximum death-rate that can be sustained without a rapid collapse of all life. But they were in a minority. If the average camp population was about six million you may be sure that not more than a million of these would be in the thirty per cent regions. Still, if that lasted for twenty years ... Let's see, eight per cent of five million over twenty years is eight million deaths. Thirty per cent of one million over twenty years is six million deaths.

At least the thirty-percenters died quickly: three months, six months, two years. Not so bad as some of the others. Imagine those of the eight-percenters that decided to survive the first year, two years, even five years. Imagine going on beyond that, hunger gnawing constantly, back-breaking work and no let-up, freezing cold, never able to savour the taste of sleep in your mouth, even for twelve years, and yet dying in the end. Not so bad.

On the whole, the labour camps were not too bad.

SOLDIERS IN TOTAL WAR, 1941-5

Ivan in the Total War Machine

Total war is (theoretically) based on the complete dedication of a nation's energies to producing the means of war, and the readiness of forces in the field to destroy the enemy's men and materials to the completest extent. Both requirements can be prepared without being fully used in practice. Indeed, since aggressors believe in quick victories, it is not, from their point of view, a question of becoming involved in total war, but of using particular methods from the total war repertory.

The state of military illusion in 1940 was ideally suited to this point of view. The First World War, it was felt, had been an error. Mechanical mobility, and a massive range of hardware, had been introduced into warfare, but it was a lumbering mobility that defeated its own ends. The railway trains carried masses of men and big guns to the front, and there they got stuck in the mud. Now . . . ah, *now !* . . . the range of transport and mechanical weapons was more efficient, adaptable and truly mobile. By delivering a series of rapid, devastating blows at the enemy, including the threat of destroying him utterly (terror), he would be demoralized and brought to his knees in the old military manner.

Exactly this was achieved in 1939/40 by the German army in Europe. However, the logic of total war had still not fully worked itself out. If a nation can become totally involved in producing the means of war, so a nation can become totally involved in resisting aggression. This is the factor that completes the logic and produces the full reality of total war.

In June 1941 two million ordinary decent Germans, instead of going to work in their city offices, factories and farms, began to cross into Russian territory. Within a few months they had occupied the Ukraine and the whole of western Russia up to Leningrad and near Moscow. In six months they had caused the deaths of about two million Russian soldiers: more than the total military deaths suffered by any nation previously in the course of an entire war.

About half of them were direct combat deaths. Of the rest, about half were prolonged deaths from the effects of wounds, and the other half from starvation and disease in prisoner-of-war camps. So that soldier-attrition now acquires the quality of civilian-attrition, in that the deaths occur on scale in a wide spectrum from immediate to prolonged dying, and from a wide variety of causes. That is the pattern of total war.

There is an alternative way of putting it. You might say that *x* thousand planes, tanks, howitzers, mortars, cans of petrol, destroyed *y* number of divisions, battalions, companies, platoons. I can only call this the *mechanthropic* vision of human events. Certainly people, or mechanthropists, will continue to have this vision. But it does create unnecessary problems in the understanding of reality. How does a mechanthropoid – an identity between machine and man – pass from a state of life to a state of death? Is it alive to begin with? And how would you describe the dissolution of a mechanthropoidal unit? ('Carnage', 'slaughter' are good, suitable, meaningless words.)

But these are needless mysteries. Let's concentrate on the human, sentimental side of things. Consider Ivan: cheerful, lucky and heroic soldier of the Red Army.

Ivan is chosen as historical representative for this episode because of his vigorous qualities. There is a duty upon us all to keep up the morale of history: how else can we ensure that the future will be just the same as the past?

Ivan had one delightful trait: he was quite unaware of his own best qualities. Before joining the army in fact he was somewhat morose and self-centred: a factory worker, earnest enough to be studying to become a draughtsman. This kept him rather apart from his workmates but he could never adapt to large groups of people anyway. Like so many of us, Ivan was suspicious and afraid of others. You could say that his wife Lenka was the only person with whom he could relax completely. Since Lenka was like himself, serious-minded and narrow in outlook, it was a joy to Ivan to be with her, to lavish affection upon her and receive it in return.

Ivan took his army training so methodically as to be well in line for promotion at the end of it, but for some reason he refused to be promoted. Maybe he was even more suspicious of those keen individuals who leap about giving and taking orders than of the crowd of lads he lived with as an ordinary soldier. At any rate Ivan stubbornly and wilfully remained a private soldier throughout his army career. He could not share his reasons with Lenka, for he knew she would have wanted him to become a sergeant. But here lies the secret of his cheerfulness. Private soldiers are by definition cheerful. You can tell that by the way they grumble all the time. They do not have the weighty responsibilities of sergeant-majors, generals and corporals. Ivan in his morose resentful way grumbled more than anyone else: you could almost say he was the most cheerful soldier in the entire Red Army.

The luck of Ivan consisted in how he managed to survive those years 1941, 1942, 1943, 1944 when more people were killed in the world than at any time before or since. If Ivan in fact only lasted till 1943, it was still a lucky achievement for a Russian soldier. His first stroke of luck was not to be amongst the three million prisoners captured by the Germans in the first six months of their onslaught. Often in modern warfare a soldier is relieved to be captured by the enemy. Bewildered by the things he is ordered to do, and realizing from experience that his chances of survival are purely random, he knows that if he is captured at least he will receive minimum rations, clothing and shelter.

In the whole course of the war the Germans took prisoner five million Russian soldiers. This is what happened to them:

Two million men were put in camps in occupied Russia; three million transferred to camps in Poland and Germany.

In Russia, almost one million of the prisoners died, mostly in conditions of total deprivation. Total deprivation of entire enclosed populations, that is to say complete exposure to weather and disease and total lack of food, does not exist elsewhere in human history.

In Germany and Poland, more than a million prisoners died in the longer-term conditions of privation, that is to say some shelter and some food in the midst of malnutrition and disease. Half a million men, in these prisoner-of-war camps in Poland and Germany, were executed by shooting.

Of the whole five million prisoners-of-war probably another half million died of exposure, disease and bullets in the course of transit from place of capture to camp, and between one camp and another.

48

One million were transferred into special anti-Russian military units or forced labour; or escaped. Another million men survived as prisoners-of-war.

Three million men died.

They were dying while lucky Ivan was at mortar practice in the heart of Russia. *Shell in-fire-phut-whizzbang-shell in-fire-phut-whizzbang-shell in* . . . He liked it. Dear Lenka, I like it . . . *fire-phut-whizzbang-shell in* . . . Not bad, really, for a factory worker. There was a certain amount of retreating to do, of course, as the Germans occupied most of European Russia. He didn't care for all that movement – mobilization, scurry, drill, columns, marching, trucks, boredom, destination anti-climax. But Ivan's unit was still in reserve, and he was able to get back to his mortar practice, the one thing he liked . . . *fire-phut-whizz-bang* . . . Dear Lenka, I must tell you about my mortar. But how to express it. How would Anton Pavlovich Chekhov have put it? . . *whizzbang-shell in-fire* . . . My dear Ivan Ivanovich! do you want my opinion as a doctor or as a writer ? . . . *phut-whizzbang* . . . There's a serious as well as a comic side to this, you know! . . . *bang-shell in-fire* . . .

Lots of men get fixed on one thing in the army. Some secretly go for banging their boots on parade, or polishing them all evening long, others get an orgasmic thrill every time they see sergeant, or get a warm cosy feel at a gun; some even enjoy saluting officers – *hup two-three sir !* There's a fetish for every-one, to hold at bay boy-scout keenness or man-brutality, those two dreaded versions of the complete soldier. Yes, there's a lot of repression of violence goes on, just like with sex. Ivan slaved away at his mortar like a pastrycook. *Bang-shell in-fire-phut-whizz* . . .

Extraordinary fortune, to be kept in reserve all through the year 1942 when so many were dying! And why did so many die? In the first place because of the shining efficiency of the new military machine and the equation it sets up between attackers and attacked. The Russians were caught on the hop by the German invasion in 1941. They were physically and psychologically unprepared. Their chief resource was numbers of men. These numbers were, in a sense, inert. Time and again vast armies were encircled by the new military machine. They were taken prisoner. They were shot up in mass by the new swiftly deployed weapons. The front armies could not retreat fast enough. Those that were able to fall back resisting expended vast numbers of men. When the Russian counter-attacks came men were used unsparingly in the mass.

It is one thing to attack into someone else's territory with the new military machine. To move forward as a pattern of machines which protect your own men as well as choosing strategies and tactics; strategies always work when they work. It is something else when the survival of a nation is under attack on the ground. There is little choosing of strategies. If men in the mass are available for resistance, they must be used. There is no choice. It only depends on the spirit of resistance. If resistance happens, it happens, and that's when working strategies stop working.

If the total resistance of all the people happens, then there is no 'objective' – no city or section of leadership – which the attacker can claim 'victory' by capturing. He has to destroy the men, and the production resources. But the Russians even moved their industry – workers, machines, entire factories – to the safe East in the face of the German advance.

So the new model army moves forward conquering all. It kills many, it cows many, it attracts collaborators. But every killing and demoralizing act stiffens the resistance of those who *will* resist and of those who have *no choice* but to resist. Until its very mobility and new efficiency have reached it up against the old logic of numbers and production in a new form. Given the spirit of total resistance and the securing of production, numbers will prevail.

Easily said! yet it can be said, easily and truly, that not only in the First World War, but in the whole of twentieth-century military evolution, the developments and advances in attacking strategies have been illusory. Only defensive warfare has developed in effective theory. There is no such thing as an effective theory of aggressive 'total war'. Total war is a machine of unpredicted event which realizes itself in the process of becoming, and from which the supremacy of defensive warfare has emerged.

In terms of Russian combat deaths (regular military) in the Second World War, the results of total war were: killed in action, five million men; died from wounds, two million men.

They say that when a cobbler is hammering away at his last, the smell of leather and tanning fills the sinuses, clots the brain with tobacco-dark fantasies. Watch a cobbler at work. Every so often his head jerks up from its thick brooding, gulps at the air and for a wild instant signals for rescue, then ducks back into the leather. How could Ivan express the absorption of a hot mortar. Dear Lenka, it's like this. *Phut-whizzbang-shell in-fire* ... Ivan chews his pencil. Why has our literature neglected the mortar? Maybe old Crime-and-Punishment would have something to say about it, something about the dark soul of Mother Russia. These are patriotic times after all, it is the Great Patriotic War.

So morose had Ivan become with his beloved mortar fumes, and with Lenka – bright, narrow-minded, perfect Lenka – so far away, that his cheerfulness knew no bounds. Lucky, cheerful Ivan. At last ...

His unit was moved into battle area, in the middle of 1943, and Ivan was at work. He loved his mortar, but this was constant overtime. *Shell in-fire-phut-whizzbang* ... And the movement was nothing like the old orderly movement of retreat. This was from here to there, backwards and forwards, set up mortar, *shell in-fire-phut-whizzbang-shell in* ... City streets, suburbs, country, it was all the same to Ivan. The noise was like one of those metal-banging factories, impressive at first then constant, seeping into the tired fabric of the body. Overtime, overtime! bending over a hot mortar, people moving all over the place. Orders. Run. Sleep two hours in abandoned house. Back on the mortar. *Phut-whizzbang* ... That heavy tiredness drags the mind down into tobacco-dark fantasies. Oven, last, banging factory, hot tube. Pastrycook, cobbler, factory worker, mortar-man Ivan.

All around him were signs of massive firepower. Buildings were burning or had burned out days ago and were black smoky shells. Some civilians still crawled about the ruins, wounded, dying of hunger, looking for lost relatives. Ivan had hardly eaten for four days, supplies were disorganized, he was dark-bearded, dirty, and his moroseness and spiteful grumbling had turned into a dark paranoia. Orders came to shift and settle, shift and settle. He had no idea whether they were advancing or retreating. Only the sound of bullets and shells gauged distance from the enemy and they were always close even if the direction and source of the fire altered. The ruined building had become safety to him, the only fixed point in a world crumbling in fire. A shell landed nearby and Ivan, prostrate before the blast, sighed with relief that it had not been a direct hit. Then the building, shaken on its last legs by the blast, began to topple. Masonry fell, before Ivan could move a great wooden beam engulfed him, crushed his legs and left his top part moaning and screaming for help.

This is how lucky, cheerful Ivan became a hero.

Historians are fond of saying 'the full toll of deaths will never be known' and so forth. But there is no mystery about Ivan's death, as you see, nor about the deaths of the other ten million Russian soldiers. The only mystery attached to Ivan is that of his life. Why did he refuse promotion? Why did he get stuck on the mortar? Did he really love Lenka? These are the bits that will never be known.

CIVILIANS IN THE SECOND
WORLD WAR, 1941–5

Lydia in the Total War Machine

LYDIA: schoolteacher, Leningrad, Autumn 1941. Age, 24, height, five feet three inches. Figure: average attractive, hips tending to bulge. Hair, long, thin, dark. Eyes, green. Features, animated, slightly lopsided, small nose.

Lydia was a very European young woman with a distinctive characteristic of extreme activity. Her strongest instincts were those of the middle class, good ones like playing a social part usefully and actively without fuss, not-so-good like a constriction of viewpoint which seems willed in contrast with the root-blindness of workers and peasants. In the middle-class sense, she was a person of qualities: stubborn, impulsive, idealistic. Most of her relatives were doctors, teachers, scientists.

Like many other Leningraders she was extremely proud of her city, of its long history as Russia's intellectual capital and the special part it played in the October revolution. She taught her pupils about how a city works, how life in a city is sustained not by accident or nature but by specific services and decisions, clinics, contacts, supplies. Sometimes she thought that the drain-consciousness she pumped into the children would not survive their leaving school: they would slump into city groups, taking things for granted, complaining about services, creating their own little heaps of human nature.

As the German attack of 1941 reached the environs of Leningrad, a note of urgency crept into Lydia's lectures. They were in demand particularly among the older children who were going to be needed, soon, as the city began to come under siege. She supplied morale as well as information. Whilst the older girls absorbed, the older boys looked at her breasts and conceived fondnesses for the rapt girls. Lydia was more enticing but less accessible.

Lydia had no vision of suffering – she was too domineering for that – but she understood the consequences of shortage and breakdown and was even able to scold people – children and adults – into actions for their own ultimate security. Yet the idea of ultimate security, in the personal sense, did not last long as the links between Leningrad and the outside world were cut off and rations dwindled to starvation level.

People turned in on themselves, personal organization crumbled. There was no security in the small human group, nor in the immediate environment except as it afforded vegetable or animal matter, things to eat, rats, leather, or things to burn in stoves against the below-zero temperature. Only the city survived. Overall organization was maintained but within that framework five thousand people every day died in the freezing months from

November to February 1942, over half a million in four months. Lydia became compassionate in her helpfulness, seeing still in gaunt dying people the structures of life and order. The compassion of the city, as expressed in dull reports, drainage systems, statistics, can achieve great things but it has its limits. Leaden skies and dull wet pavements, snow left in the streets along with collapsed bodies of men and women. The environment is stripped of sustenance, narrows, moves in on the body with brittle cold. The body feeds on itself, passes from warmth through shrinking panic to a grinding tastelessness. Organs wither and hurt in their unfed fluids. The trick of life: strong and enduring, it can nevertheless be pressured to a frail snapping-point where the final cry is barely audible. Forget about heroic endurance, physical horrors and other bombast. Listen for the small sounds of a million people dying.

Leningrad 1941–3 was the first living city to become a city of the dead. As at Verdun in 1916, half a million people died in the first four months of onslaught – of hunger and disease as against shells and bullets – followed by a year's straggling attrition bringing the total dead to over one million.

As Verdun, the Somme and the rest were metropolises in a wider area of death, so Leningrad was a concentration of one million out of a total of ten million civilian deaths diffused over Russia 1941–5.

The two big wars of our century have a broad pattern or rhythm in common, inherent in the scale of operations: the initial series of attacks bringing massive loss of lives; the 'bogged down' period of combat lasting several years and causing the major attrition of human life; and the period of final retreat and withdrawal.

We may adapt this pattern to the case of the civilian population of Russia in the Second World War.

Phase 1. Advance of the invading armies. Six months, June–December 1941

Bombing of towns and cities was part of the terrorizing attack, as well as killing old ladies and other roadside refugees with machine-guns fired from aeroplanes ('strafing' as it is joy-fully called).

Probably most deaths amongst refugees were from the immed-iate effects of exposure and starvation. Large collections of people found themselves in strange towns being caught up by the invaders, unable to move on, waiting in captive but neglected groups where disease was added to hunger and homelessness.

When towns were occupied, and even some villages, a small number of potential troublemakers were immediately shot or hanged; 'troublemakers' of course being those people, officials and political commissars, who kept order before the invaders arrived.

All of these types of violence probably accumulated to about half a million civilian deaths in the short brilliant surge of the military machine.

Phase 2. Occupation by the invader. Between two and three years, 1941–4

In the occupation period the logic of the total-war machine completes itself. Not in random atrocities such as make scandals in the newspapers but in the application to the civilian popula-tion of the same pressure which is the theme of the military war: attrition.

The scale of disruption in Soviet towns and cities is indicated by the fact that many of them, at liberation, contained between one-half and one-third only of their pre-war populations. The initial drainage is accounted for by population movements. On the basis of twenty million people in towns in the occupied area: about two million would be in the armed forces; probably around two million left the towns, including those who fled out of the occupied area, those who joined partisan units and workers moving east with their factories. Four million people were deported as slave labour to Germany. Altogether, forty per cent or eight million people.

About forty per cent were left in the towns at liberation, and something in the region of twenty per cent died in the process of attrition during occupation. My own estimate is four and a half million.

About three million of these people, containing a preponderance of old people, women and children, died from want and neglect. Rations were meagre, and often subject to arbitrary lowering or complete cutting-off by the occupying administrators. Apart from weakened resistance to common ailments through lack of food, disease often reached epidemic level and hunger often reached famine level.

One million people were killed because they were Jews.

About half a million people were executed over the period because they were political commissars or officials, saboteurs or partisan suspects. There was also a good deal of killing for killing's sake. In South Russia some thousands of old people were killed on the pretext of 'euthanasia'.

Deaths in the villages are not so easy to estimate. I have assumed that the slow attrition of hunger did not operate in the villages, on the principle that food producers have to be kept alive (an example of Nazi idealism). Thousands of villages were destroyed, burnt and the inhabitants shot as 'reprisals' for partisan activities. The partisans themselves were shot when captured. It is easy to exaggerate the accumulated total of deaths occurring in a multiplicity of small groups. Nevertheless it seems likely that the total number of peasants and partisans, shot and dying in the immediate privation of homelessness, was at least one million, a majority peasants in their homes rather than partisans, and most of them actually shot.

The numbers accumulate ... There is always uncertainty about the exact figures in a massive area of death. But when you look at the available evidence for each different *type* of death in turn, the numbers accumulate to an unshakeably correct order of magnitude.

We now have five and a half million in the towns and villages in the occupation period; plus the half million deaths in the invasion period and the one million who died in Leningrad. Seven million civilian deaths in the periods of invasion and occupation.

Phase 3. Retreat and withdrawal of the invader. One year, 1943–4

The violence of the invader army towards the civilian popula-

56

tion was more severe in the retreating phase than it had been in the period of advance. In the course of the war eight million Russian houses were destroyed, and a high proportion of these were during the withdrawal from Russia. Crops and livestock were destroyed on a vast scale. Special systems and machines were used to destroy crops in seed, and growing crops were burned. Spring and summer.

Before leaving the towns and villages the invaders commonly put to death the prisoners they had on hand in their jails. This was not a new phenomenon. In Moscow in 1920, when the death penalty was abolished, the Moscow secret police in one night executed a large proportion of their prisoners, presenting the government in the morning with a *fait accompli*. One writer has called this 'liquidating their stock': a case of 'occupational psychosis'. Here of course the psychosis and the killings were on a vaster scale.

It is likely that in the immediate privation of wrecked homes, destroyed crops and livestock and purloined food supplies, and in the farewell executions, about one million people died.

'Aftermath' is supposed to mean stubbled fields and store-houses packed with grain. In the aftermath of this wreckage, the death environment created over three years by the invader army, and their parting blows of destruction, probably at least another two million people died in Russian towns and villages over the next year or so, from slow privation.

Only two seasons, spring and summer, were destroyed by the invaders. Maybe they had a go at autumn as well. The one thing they never managed to destroy was the Russian winter.

LYDIA: citizen of Leningrad, winter 1943. Age 26, features dull, listless. Figure: emaciated, abdomen tending to bulge. Eyes, sunken. Distinguishing characteristics: withered lips, sores round mouth.

Lydia has joined that great fellowship of the twentieth century: those with death-in-the-eyes.

The types of violence perpetrated on Russian civilians in the Second World War give us a pyramid similar to that of the Russian Civil War period:

DEATHS

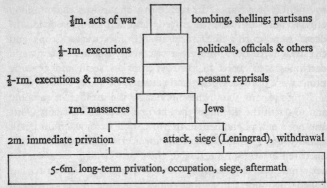

½m. acts of war — bombing, shelling; partisans

½-1m. executions — politicals, officials & others

½-1m. executions & massacres — peasant reprisals

1m. massacres — Jews

2m. immediate privation — attack, siege (Leningrad), withdrawal

5-6m. long-term privation, occupation, siege, aftermath

HARD VIOLENCE: Estimate 2-3 million deaths

PRIVATION: Estimate 7-8 million deaths

The difference between the two is in the technologies used to kill and, bound up with that, in the type of consciousness involved in producing death. I described the death-breeding machine of the Civil War years as beginning from initially remote pressures – the First World War, the revolutionary attitude and reactions to it – which produced a series of vacuums in society. These vacuums sucked away the life-sustaining capacities of the urban society. In terms of hard violence, there was some conventional military violence; violent error and violent deprivation produced confused man-to-man killings; there was some violence by professional death-men (secret police) but on a scale small in relation to later developments. The death-breeding machine, in part the product of the violent consciousness, was in greater measure the manufacturer of violent consciousness for the future.

The total-war machine of the Second World War was very different, and a much more conscious process. The new military machine brought the terror of military hardware into the heart of civilian life (bombing and shelling), and used it against the resistance which it evoked (partisans, peasant reprisals). The military machine secured the occupation of foreign towns and cities and allowed the acts of execution and massacre committed by civil and military administrations (on politicals, officials and others); and the acts of massacre committed by the professional death-men (secret police killings of Jews). The military machine committed the acts of military terror, of total city-siege, of destroying the means of life which led to the immediate-privation, deaths of civilians during the attack, the siege of Leningrad, and the military withdrawal. The civil and military occupation administrations supposedly stimulated by Nazi ideology and anti-Slav racism, were in a total situation which, in realistic terms and irrespective of ideology and racism, could not possibly fail to cause long-term privation to millions; and to this fact they added their own inefficiencies and corruptions.

And back in eastern, central and western Europe, the total-war machine held down populations for the operation of the European version of the total state machine: the death-camps of Nazi Germany and German-occupied Poland.

4

CHINA IN THE
TWENTIETH CENTURY

Wang in the Total War Machine

THE great change that has occurred in the twentieth century, as perceivable in the changing modes of violence, is the transformation of men living in a 'natural' environment, with a hesitant consciousness of social relationships, into men living in a 'man-made' environment, with an acute consciousness of social relationships.

There is a lot more to be said on this subject with regard to Europe and Russia. In the case of China, certain aspects of the transformation stand out in violent relief from the general world picture. The most intense difference is the original environment, and the type of consciousness, from which the Chinese people have progressed.

In the nineteenth century the Chinese Empire reached its lowest level of decadence. Alienation between classes – landlords, administrators on the one hand, peasants on the other – was complete. There were cases of upper-class people having lampshades made out of the skin of dead peasants – a symbol of dehumanized relationships which in Europe was only achieved at the peak of massive technological organization and conscious racist ideology, when in the early 1940s some Nazi ladies did the same with the skin of dead Jews. Furthermore, the Chinese landscape, which afforded a wretched subsistence to peasants at the best of times, was subject to recurrent drought causing famine and death, and recurrent floods from the overflowing of river banks. The natural environment was thus intermittently violent, and a regular provider of malnutrition and disease. In the 1850s fighting broke out in some Chinese provinces. The violence accumulated, in association with drought and flood, to an extent which has been estimated at the loss of eighty million lives. For a demographic catastrophe on this scale, in pre-twentieth-century Europe, you have to go back to the Thirty Years War in the early seventeenth century, or the Black Death of the middle ages.

The Chinese Imperial authority, such as it was, was toppled in 1911 in the Sun-Yat-Sen revolution, and Republican China came into being. But Sun-Yat-Sen did not succeed in establishing a new political authority. His Kuomintang disintegrated into the local rule of its provincial administrators and military governors. The period of 'warlord' rule, when no effective central authority existed, lasted into the mid-1920s. Then the idea of a central Kuomintang revived. By 1927 the Kuomintang under Chiang Kai-shek, and with the help of the Communists who were already organizing peasant associations in the villages, had established a kind of central authority. In that year also the final split occurred between the Kuomintang and the Communists. Thus 1927 dates the beginning of the Chinese Civil War in the sense of the struggle for power between Communists and Kuomintang.

To quantify the violence in China in the warlord period, up to about 1927, is a job for demographers; it's beyond me. But the *shape* of violence in that period is clear enough. The warlords fought among themselves, like bandits. Their local regimes were corrupt and self-seeking. They imposed a pretty brutal man-to-man relationship on the people. You might call it a 'natural' kind of violence, without the intrusion or influence of large man-made technologies or ideologies. From the point of view of the people, to the existing wretchedness and violence of the natural environment was added an extra dimension of brutality in their relationships with the powers-that-be.

A comparison between Russia and China in the twentieth century is inevitable. Both began it with decadent empires. Both had a major Communist revolution, a civil war, and were affected by world war. But it's the differences that are most revealing. The Russian Empire broke up amid the massive disruptions of the First World War. The Russian Civil War happened *after* the revolution and the installation of the Communist state; the scale of violence was affected by the world war and the attitudes of an entrenched regime. Violence in Russia after the Civil War was organized with the technologies of the total state, both the internal system of secret police and labour camps, and, in the Second World War, the massive military technologies of total war.

In China the downfall of the Imperial dynasty was not accompanied by any effective efforts at transformation. For fifteen years the corrupt pressures which the people had known under the Empire were merely intensified under the warlords. The Kuomintang-Communist civil war, between 1927 and 1937, was characterized by terror-killing reflecting the ideological attitudes typical of the twentieth century, and large loss of life through privation. But total-war methods, in the modern technological sense, were used only by the Japanese during the Sino-Japanese war of 1937–45. The resumption of the Kuomintang-Communist conflict in 1945 brought full-scale civil war until the Communist victory in 1949 and the installation of the Communist state. There was one episode of massive state killing, in 1951.

Thus the major violence in China occurred *before* the formal revolution and the existence of the total state. The technologies of state violence did not operate as they did in Russia, except in the form of the Japanese invader and in the executions of 'enemies of the people' in 1951.

The other major difference is that in China the deaths, in the military sense, were mainly in the countryside and, in the sense of civilian privation, chiefly in the villages. Chiefly in the villages and, as the elocutionists say, mainly on the plains, we can see the evolving shapes of violence in China in the period 1927–51:

Phase 1. Kuomintang-Communist Civil War, first period, 1927–30
This period is characterized not so much by confrontation of armies as by political violence on both sides. The Kuomintang

under Chiang Kai-shek launched a terror against Communists in the towns; the Communists under Mao Tse-tung were killing landlords in the countryside, leading peasant insurrections, establishing guerrilla bases in South China, particularly in Kiangsi where a Soviet Republic was later proclaimed. It is unlikely the killing reached demographic proportions. More likely it was on the scale of the public terror of the Russian Civil War: up to about 50/100,000 deaths. The Communist army was small, growing in the period to about 30,000 men.

Phase 2. Kuomintang-Communist Civil War, second period, 1930–37

The Communist tactics were to develop political consciousness among the peasants in the areas where they had guerrilla bases, and to augment their armies from discontented peasants. The Kuomintang carried out a series of 'bandit extermination' campaigns against the Communist guerrillas and their peasant sympathizers in South China. Apart from direct killings, the disruption caused great privation among the peasants.

By 1934 the Kuomintang had cleared the Communists out of the short-lived Soviet Republic of Kiangsi. The Communist army began its famous 'Long march' to North China, lasting one year, under constant harassment from Kuomintang armies. Again, the disruption left a trail of privation deaths in the villages.

Over the period, military deaths were of the order of 100,000. Deaths among the peasants, from direct killing, starvation and other forms of privation, are estimated at between one and two million.

The Communists now had a secure base in North China, from which they could 'liberate' surrounding areas. The army had grown to over 100,000, although less than a third of these survived the long march and reached North China.

Phase 3. Sino-Japanese War, 1937–45. South China

The Chinese armies were no match for the mechanized Japanese in conventional warfare. When the southern, Kuomintang armies offered resistance to the invaders at Shanghai and

63

Nanking, they were massacred, as were many civilians in those cities. At least half a million soldiers and civilians were killed in the first six months. Millions of Chinese fled westward from the coastal cities.

By 1939 the invader armies had occupied the main cities, the coast of China from north to south, and the Chinese countryside in some depth. Along a straggling front of two thousand miles up and down Central and South China, the opposing armies were separated by a wide belt of despoiled countryside. The invaders, a few hundred thousand at maximum, were entrenched in villages with artillery and machine-guns. The main Chinese armies, numbering millions, were poorly equipped and organized. For virtually the rest of the war, combat was confined to minor engagements in the no-man's land between the armies. The invaders had initially penetrated the countryside with terrorizing attacks on villages, burning, raping and killing. Throughout the war they continued such practices with raids on the villages lying between the armies.

The total result was six or seven years of static attrition, not so much in combat deaths as in malnutrition and starvation in the Chinese armies; compounded by a series of droughts in the early 1940s bringing large-scale famine.

Phase 4. Sino-Japanese War, 1937–45. North China

In North China things were different. The Communist armies, from the bases secured and widened after the long march, offered troublesome resistance to the invaders from the start. Prolonged frontal resistance was impracticable, however, and Mao's armies split up into smaller guerrilla units which within a few years increased the Communist-held parts of North China from a population area of one million to an area of forty million people.

Mao's long-term view was that the revolution must happen in the first place in the villages. Hence peasant allegiance, and peasant willingness to join his forces, were necessary for the purposes of the revolution as well as for the immediate task of combating the invaders. Up to 1941 this Communist purpose was only partially successful: by then the Communist-held area had been reduced again, by Japanese actions, to an area of twenty million people.

Mao had expressed the Communists' reliance on the peasants in the phrase, 'The peasants are the ocean in which the Red Army swims.' In 1941 the Japanese commanders decided to oppose the Red Army by a policy of 'draining the ocean'.

Perhaps the implications of 'draining the ocean' in an area of twenty million people are worth a few moments' reflection ...

The means of draining the ocean was the Japanese 'three-all' strategy, meaning 'loot-all, burn-all, kill-all'; or, in less colourful Western terms, total war upon the peasants in the villages. During part of 1941, and 1942, the invaders carried out a systematic operation of burning crops, killing peasants in the villages or leaving them to die of starvation in burnt-out villages set in a ravaged landscape. Peasant families who fled to the hills were pursued. Many were destroyed by gassing in large hill-caves, where they had found refuge. A drought bringing famine to some areas of North China completed the devastation of 1942.

Among those who survived, the result of this total-war strategy was to stiffen peasant resistance and to achieve decisively for the Communists what their own efforts had only tentatively begun to achieve: the allegiance of the peasants. The peasants became responsive to Communist efforts to revolutionize the villages, and they joined the Communist armies in large numbers.

By the end of the war the parts of North China 'liberated' by the Communists had grown to a population area of nearly one hundred million. In large parts of this area the villages had been revolutionized – that is the land re-distributed and the village politically re-organized for the future. And the Red Army had grown from fewer than a hundred thousand at the beginning of the war to over one million at the end of it: a highly motivated fighting force ready for the final struggle for power with the Kuomintang.

Deaths in the Sino-Japanese war, or the Second World War in China, were of the order of fifteen million, a majority of these occurring in North China. Direct killings, military and civilian, would be at least two million. Probably a figure of at least three million died from the immediate privations suffered by refugees fleeing from the cities at the beginning of the war; by peasants whose villages were destroyed during the Japanese advances into south and central China, and in destructive raids during the occupation of these areas; and by peasants who suffered the destructions of the three-all policy in North China as well as the wider ravages in that area throughout the war. Up to ten million died in all China from slow privation. In addition to this, probably another five million died from famine in the droughts of the early 1940s.

Old Wang was one of those who survive in troubled times by keeping on the right side of people in their own prickly, uncompromising way. Even thirty years before, when his children were already grown up and working in the fields, Wang was well in with the landlord – unaccountably so, since he was one of the poorest peasants in the village and on the face of it had nothing to offer to the superior classes apart from a surly assertion of his own existence. Nevertheless, during the years of decline into old age, Wang 'prospered'; that is to say, he did not starve, nor did he suffer humiliation from those strangers who came at different times to assert their authority in the village. He never joined in communal complaints about drought and bad harvests. He mocked the fears of others when there were rumours of hostile strangers in the vicinity. What's the difference who comes to the village, his attitude seemed to say – they'll be no worse than you lot. Wang continued apparently to eat the same meagre amount through drought and requisition; to follow the same routines no matter what strangers were lording it in the village. He outlived and outstayed most of his own progeny.

Inevitably, stories about Wang built up over the years. It was said that he had acquiesced in a daughter-in-law being taken off for the pleasure of a warlord official; that he had failed to comfort his son or try to prevent him from leaving the village with his young family, in his sorrow, for an uncertain future. It was 'known for a fact' that he'd encouraged his two unmarried sons to join 'bandit armies', not for political reasons but so that they would not be a burden on his tiny plot of land. It was rumoured that he had refused help to his children's families when they were starving. It was even whispered that when his wife died it was because Wang deprived her of food when she was ill, during a bad harvest season. He was said to be a friend of the warlords, a protected Communist when the Reds were taking food off other villagers, a collaborator when the Japanese passed through.

Whatever the truth of all this, Wang kept his mysteries wrapped up in himself. He certainly pecked and scolded at invaders, guerrillas, officials in the same querulous old voice he used on his fellow-villagers. He was capable of haranguing people in the street without warning, especially criticizing young people in terms of the habits of their forebears whom he'd long outlived and whom they themselves had hardly known. He was an isolated old man. One of his sons still lived with his family on the other side of the village, but they'd been estranged for years. In a close community it can take a lifetime to walk two hundred yards!

When it was rumoured that the Japanese were coming again, in 1942, Wang watched the villagers' reactions with astonishment. Suddenly the quiet little place was like a busy city thoroughfare. Everyone was out in the open. Stories were spreading round: the fields were being laid waste – houses burnt – people killed. Wang stood in his doorway, watching them. Some were saddling up mules, some were assembling bundles in carts, others were just rushing about. They were leaving the village! Wang kept his voice to a low mutter, a commentary on the habits of those people he had known so well from such a distance for so long, who were now preparing to run like mice across a burning field. Someone came running up to him as the throng began to move out of the village, others rushing to catch up. It was his son. Wang looked at him with contempt. He pretended not to hear his entreaties, to come with them, to forget the past, to be a father, to flee. Wang spat on the ground, with all the vigour he could muster. His son turned away – and fled, like all the rest.

After they'd all gone, Wang began to tremble. He was very old. He watched a space between the trees, on the pathway high above the village, until the first slow-moving refugees appeared.

He began to yell at them then, shaking his fist, denouncing. But he couldn't keep that up for long. It only made him tremble the more. He could only stand still in his doorway, an old man half in the sun, half in the shadow of his own house. Finally he saw the soldiers approaching. He shook with impatience until he was sure they were within earshot, then let fly at them. He let loose every angry denunciation that came into his head – not of the soldiers, but of the foolish villagers. Two of the soldiers came towards him – little men with blank faces. One struck at him with his rifle-butt. The other kicked him as he fell. They went away. Wang lay just inside his house. He was still conscious, but he was too old to get up under the pain. The detachment of soldiers scattered methodically among the houses and began to set fire to them.

Phase 5. Kuomintang-Communist Civil War, final period, 1945–9

The Civil War resumed as military confrontation of a type which had not existed before between the two sides. The Communists, with an area of the country of a hundred million people firmly under their control, and with an experienced and highly motivated army of a million men, eventually defeated the Kuomintang, or 'Chinese Nationalist' army, numbering several millions: heavily supplied by the Americans but nevertheless ill-organized. Military deaths were on the scale of half a million to one million men.

Phase 6. Demographic violence in the villages, 1943–9

During the Sino-Japanese, and the final phase of the Civil War, as the Communist armies 'liberated' progressively wider areas of the country, people were sent into the villages to carry out basic political re-organization and redistribution of the land: 'bringing the revolution to the village'. The new village associations began on a wide scale around 1943. This was followed by a series of 'campaigns' or practical directives, issued from the Communist centre and promulgated to the villages by the usual means of communication and intended to direct political action on specific issues. Notable among these were: the Anti-Traitor movement of 1945, designed to punish people who had fought for the Japanese in puppet-Kuomintang armies against the Chinese in the North; and the Settling Accounts movement of 1946. The latter was a series of three directives spaced over 1946 advocating 'struggle against the landlords' and, specifically, expropriation of landlords' property by the peasants' village associations.

The directives did not advocate violence. In the event, they resulted in landlords being beaten, some being beaten to death; in some landlord's families being beaten to death; in the extension of the 'settling accounts' principle to some who were not landlords but who had accounts; and, in villages where there were Communist militia-men with weapons and, at that stage, little supervision from outside, in a certain amount of shooting. In other words, this is almost certainly an example of like-minded violent behaviour occurring on a demographic scale, in 'every village', similar to the violence of the Poor Peasants Committees in Russia in 1918. Occurring as it did in an area of a hundred million people, it is not outrageous to suggest that the deaths from this kind of action would be of the order of one million in number.

Steps were later taken to prevent the recurrence of this kind of violence.

Phase 7. Post-revolutionary state violence, 1951

Two years after the Communist victory and takeover of the state, it was announced that a large number had been tried and executed as 'enemies of the people'. Observers' estimates have put the figure at about two million people.

Apart from this, there is no evidence that internal state violence in China has developed in any large-scale fashion. It will be remembered that in Russia the massive state violence of Stalinism began with the collectivization of the peasants, an operation that was carried out from the beginning in a spirit of hostility and violence. In China, the revolution from the beginning was founded partly on the co-operation of the peasants, partly on the persuasion of the peasants based on an effective political structure in the villages.

To get a proper picture of deaths in twentieth-century China due to the hostile environment – natural and man-made – would take a full-scale demographic history. You would start with the average life-expectancy of peasants under Imperial rule – probably about thirty years or less. Or, to put this idea in more graspable terms, for every person that survived into old age, several died in childhood, in youth, or in later hardships. You would have to decide how far the high death-rate was due to lack of medical skill in combatting disease and ordinary illnesses; and how much it was augmented by natural disasters such as flood and famine. A look at the nature of the land would give you some ideas on the inherent possibilities of getting a living from the land the peasants actually worked. Then you would ask to what extent these possibilities were held back by the existing social organization: not only the rule of landlords but also the practice of inherited land being divided up among sons to the point where it could not give a living to their families.

You would realize that the mixture of natural and man-made conditions leading to early death lasted right up to the formal revolution of 1949. And to what extent were these existing conditions exacerbated by the further man-made pressures of the intervening years: the rule of the warlords, the technologies of war – civil and inter-state – the sudden advent of new forms of social organization and the first actions of the new state? That would be the big, final question.

I imagine that in carrying out such a study (as I hope you will) you will acquire a pretty sophisticated notion of the difference between a natural environment and a man-made environment. You will avoid the mistake of thinking it's the same as the difference between a rural life and a city life, or agriculture and industry. Clearly the man-made influence is at work in even the most primitive form of country living and rural economy. Equally, you won't be taken in by the suggestion that an environment can be entirely man-made, in the conscious sense. For this reason you wouldn't expect, for example, that China, being taken over in 1949 by a new and highly conscious man-made theory of social organization, would be able to transform the conditions of living, and dying, overnight, or even in a short period of time.

What I have tried to do in this chapter is something much cruder than what might be made possible by the kind of study suggested above. I have merely tried to identify the scale and types of death which were *undeniably* man-made. Also, I am taking a much broader view of the difference between the natural and the man-made environment. This is simply that before the twentieth century people *believed* they lived in a 'natural' environment, whether in town or country, where everything was in its proper place. Not entirely true, but largely so. However, the other end of the proposition can be more definitely asserted. Only in our century has the world of men claimed that the environment of the generality of people *can* be man-made. It is a difference in consciousness.

5

THE JEWS OF
EUROPE

Stan in the Total Death Machine (1)

STAN worked as a presser in a little clothing factory in central
Poland. A small dark man with an oval face rather like that of a
timid child, Stan was strikingly unlike the blond, muscularly
swelling giants who worked in Aryan clothing factories for the
same wages. Every Friday a representative of the Beth Din
visited his house and took blood samples of Stan, his wife Suzi
and their small children Michael and Rachel. This was to ensure
that their blood was strictly kosher, or at least sufficiently so to
get them through the Sabbath without infection to the soul. In
the same sense, the gorgeous Aryan garment workers had blood
samples taken, also on a Friday, to ensure that the milk they
gave was free from impurities and suitable for fastidious house-
wives. This was known as tuberculin-testing, a scientific means
of implanting a golden dawn of promise in the hearts of men, or
at any rate in the hearts of Aryans. The kosher blood-sampling,
on the other hand, was essentially a secret ritual, basically dark
and alien, and fundamentally designed to subvert, essentially,
humanity.

As a matter of fact, this particular fairy-tale was not part of
Stan's repertory of witticism, since he had never heard of
Aryans. His favourite joke was that he did the sweating for the
sweat-shop. True enough: he worked, pressing, in a habitual
cloud of steam, shirt-sleeves flying, the back of his neck red with
a perpetual trickle of sweat. It was worth it, for the kids. Most of
his hope as a man was fixed on little Michael and Rachel,
although according to his wife Suzi it ought to be fixed on his

own 'advancement'. Suzi's brother Sidney was successful in import-export, a fact she never let him forget. To Stan, the idea that he could better himself (objective reality again!) was ridiculous. He made veiled references to it at work. Not that he'd bring his quarrels with Suzi into the sewing-shop but he'd look through his cloud of steam at his workmates on their benches and yell, 'Imagine me with a big cigar and offices in three cities!' and their laughter would be for him a secret dig at Suzi. When brother-in-law Sidney exported himself to America, in the summer of 1939, Stan sighed with relief. Now he could relax, and think what a fine fellow little Michael would be when he grew up, a scholar perhaps, and how Rachel would bring home men who ought to be ashamed to be seen talking to a garment worker.

Soon after this, the invaders came into Poland. Stan and his workmates were told they were to be moved to another town; their jobs and houses were to be taken over by 'racial Germans'. A racial German was something very complex and scientific, rather like the tuberculin-tested Aryans, and quite beyond Stan's understanding. He tried to imagine a queue of racial Germans lining up in eagerness for his job, and what the successful applicant would be like. Wiping the back of his neck with a sweat-rag for the last time, Stan could only mutter, 'At this he won't stay fat for long.'

Life in the new ghetto was not a bit likeable. Stan was back on garments, stitching and sewing now. They had to march to work, Suzi as well, and living was in dormitories and they had to queue up for food. At work there were guards, at home . . . in the dormitory there were rabbis and people who organized things. Stan was rather sour towards all those who hovered about in authority, perhaps a way of keeping them at a distance, while Suzi complained about the black markets in food and about the way people behaved in general. Stan was irritated by having to think about the wicked things some people did because it seemed less important than the way everyone around them was becoming unrecognizable through hunger. It was as if someone was trying to prove that people are no good in any way at all. When one of the children had a fever there was a wretched temptation not to seek the medical help the organizers tried to provide but to see the illness as part of the surroundings, let it sink deeper into the hollows of the kid's eyes ... If an old woman died in the dormitory there was the same grudging uncertainty as to whether to dole out a little sympathy or just let it pass ... About a year went by in this way. During a typhus epidemic in a neighbouring district someone mentioned that people were dying like flies. Stan was still able to be shocked by the phrase.

It's said that some primitive tribes call their children insulting names so that they will appear worthless to evil spirits who are looking for a bit of worth. We do the same, of course, with our own civilized children. But Stan couldn't bring himself to the point of seeing his Rachel and his Michael as insects. They won't die like flies, he thought.

Authority never lets you know when you are to die, except when you are a convicted murderer. But when authority is the murderer there is no official notification. Stan and his family and his dormitory and his ghetto area were lined up and marched to the railway station. They filed into a closed cattle truck. For forty-eight hours while the train followed its instructions Stan stood, or existed, between other bodies; Suzi and the kids sat and lay somewhere at his feet. When the door of the waggon finally slid open Stan perceived, as the crowd carried him toward the doorway, that Rachel and Michael were dead and Suzi, alive, was not getting to her feet. He was carried toward the light and air. For a moment he had free space to descend from the waggon. As he descended a machine-gun bullet hit his body.

There are two kinds of total-death machine. One is the system of the atom and hydrogen bombs. What makes that a total-death machine is the hardware of the system – the exploding bomb itself. The other kind of total-death machine is the system which crushed the Jews of Europe. The 'hardware' of that system is, as we all know, gas-chambers and guns. But that system is not primarily dependent upon its hardware. What makes it a total-death machine is the *organization* of the system, or, in our modern language, the software technology. That is the important difference between the two kinds of total death machine.

Unlike the Russian labour camps, the German death camp system is not a case of internal state violence. The death camps were situated outside Germany, in Poland. Only five per cent of the Jews who died were Germans.

In parenthesis, I must introduce here a concept which is essential to the understanding of large-scale violent death. When we measure people in percentages we are usually dealing with a very limited aspect of their lives – their desire for housing, voting intentions, purchasing behaviour. So we can usually afford to marginalize certain minorities – the twenty per cent who have to wait for a house, the unimportant five per cent fascist vote, the trivial two per cent who don't buy Bippo – without being unduly harsh or inhuman in our attitudes. In measuring deaths there are no such relativities. We are measuring the complete human being, the end of his life. So, in saying five per cent of the Jews who died were Germans, we are not referring to a margin who were better off, worse off, suffered slightly more than others: we are saying that a quarter of a million of the Jews who died happened to be Germans. In measuring deaths, every percentage point is an absolute.

Only a quarter of a million were Germans. About a million came from Western and South-East Europe, a million died in Russia and the Baltic States; the rest, about two and a half million, were Polish. Between four and five million Jews died in the system.

Clearly, not an internal state system. But it was a projection of the total-state system of Germany under the Nazis. The system was projected, carried into the countries occupied by the German military machine. The people who ran the system were somewhat more extended than the Russian secret police who ran the labour camps. They were a secret police with their own military arm, working in close co-operation with the main military machine which made their operations possible. Obviously this total-death machine has a diffuse aspect to it, a reaching-out into far-flung territories; and a concentrated aspect which we call the death camps and the enclosed ghettoes.

Let's start at the concentrated heart of the operative system. Just step over the border from Germany into Poland. Draw a line from Chelmno in the north to Auschwitz in the south, at that corner of Poland enclosed by Germany and Czechoslovakia: 180 miles. From each of these points project a line eastward into Poland: Chelmno-Treblinka, 150 miles; Auschwitz-Belsec, 170 miles. You have two almost parallel lines. Still bearing east, bring the lines in fairly sharply to meet at Sobibor: Treblinka-Sobibor, 105 miles; Belsec-Sobibor, 100 miles. There you have the pentagon of the death camps. Chelmno, Auschwitz, Treblinka, Belsec, Sobibor.

Inside the pentagon, in the northern half, there is a flat triangle formed by Lodz-to-Lublin as the base, and Warsaw as the apex. This is the triangle of the main enclosed ghettoes. Outside Lublin city, in the region of Lublinland, is a general concentration of Jews, in roughly that bit of the pentagon that narrows in to Sobibor. Also near Lublin is a place called Maidanek concentration camp.

Inside the pentagonal area, and in the death camps at its five points, died about half of all the Jews who fell victim to the total-death machine. In the ghetto regions of that area were one to one and a half million people. Ghettoes had already existed, but in the early years of occupation many extra people were moved in, from Eastern Poland (like Stan) and from Germany and Austria, in a general attempt to concentrate Jewish people in one area. Over the years, more than half of these people died from the various forms of privation: hunger, disease, famine, forced labour. In those worst years for the world, 1941, 1942, 1943 and 1944, the ghettoes were at various times 'cleared' or partially cleared. That is to say, large numbers of the surviving inhabitants were sent to the death camps by train, there to be put to death by asphyxiation in gas chambers or gas vans.

If you look at the map you will see there is an obvious positional relationship between the ghettoes and particular death camps: Lodz-Chelmno; Warsaw-Treblinka; Lublin-Sobibor, Belsec. Since the largest ghetto was Warsaw (half a million people at one point), and the largest 'clearance' was made from there, it follows that of these death camps Treblinka was the one where most people were gassed: probably about three hundred thousand. Maidanek concentration camp near Lublin was also used partly as a death camp, so that in the Maidanek-Sobibor-Belsec complex, and at Chelmno, a further number of people, in the region of two hundred thousand, were killed by gas fumes.

A concentration camp is a place where people are held prisoner, where they may have to do forced labour, and where they die of various privations. A death camp is a place where people are killed. Auschwitz was a concentration camp, used partly as a death camp. The death camp proper was the neighbouring camp of Birkenau. About a million people were killed by gassing at Auschwitz-Birkenau. Again looking at the map, you will see that it is somewhat distanced from the main ghetto-death camp arrangement. Auschwitz was used for killing people sent there in trains from the far-flung territories occupied by the German armies. Half a million Rumanian and Hungarian Jews died. A large proportion of these died in their own countries, but many went to Auschwitz. From France and the Low Countries, one hundred thousand, from Czechoslovakia, Yugoslavia and Greece, one hundred thousand, from the Baltic States and Eastern Poland, two hundred thousand, all went to Auschwitz.

To locate the other half of the Jews that died, blow your mind eastward through Poland, the Baltic States and into the heart of Russia. In the existing ghettoes of these regions at least another two million died. About a million people were shot. They were shot up in ghettoes or rounded up for firing squads. In some places such as Babyi Yar near Kiev people were systematically shot and covered with earth, shot and covered with earth, in vast execution pits. Probably more than a million people died of privation in these regions.

In all, about a million and a half people were gassed, a million were shot, and two million or more died of hunger, disease, forced labour conditions and the privations of forced travel in the open and in railway waggons.

If the total-death machine was run with the 'cold, inhuman efficiency' that is so often advertised as its hallmark, how is it we are uncertain whether the total number of deaths was four million or five million? The answer is that it was not particularly efficient, it was merely organizational.

During the early transfers of people from Eastern Poland, Germany and Austria into the ghettoes of Lodz, Lublin and Warsaw, the movement of people was chaotic, and thousands died of exposure and hunger. In later years people were moved across Poland in either direction in patterns of total meaninglessness.

The idea of gassing people grew from the existing practice of 'euthanasia' in Nazi Germany, by which science, thousands of aged and sick people had already been killed. There was no euthanasia in the total-death machine. 'Euthanasia' means 'a quiet and easy death'. It can be said with some certainty that of all those five million people, not a single one died a quiet and easy death. We are reminded, in contradiction to the usual myth of 'nameless and anonymous masses', that there is not a single human being in the world who does not have a name: an efficiency of peaceful living that cannot be obscured by violence and its pretensions.

The first people gassed, at Chelmno, were killed in sealed vans into which was pumped the carbon monoxide fumes from the motor engine. The system constantly broke down, as it did in Russia where the same method was used. Carbon monoxide fumes, pumped into specially built chambers, were used at Belsec, Treblinka and Sobibor. There were rebellions and mutinies at Treblinka and Sobibor. At Treblinka, when the trains from Warsaw were arriving in 1942, the waggons were so packed with people that thousands died from suffocation on the journey. When the gas chambers could not cope with the numbers arriving, people (like Stan) were machine-gunned as they came out of the waggons. At Chelmno in 1944 the mass graves were opened and attempts made to 'destroy the evidence' by burning the bodies soaked in petrol.

At Auschwitz-Birkenau Cyclone B crystals – a disinfecting agent giving off poisonous fumes – were used from 1943 onwards when trains were arriving from the far-flung territories controlled by the German army. In that place also thousands died in punishment commandos and from destitution as well as in the gas chambers.

The movement of 'racial Germans' into areas vacated by Polish Jews – the actuality of *lebensraum* and of those myths about 'population pressure' still so eagerly spread by theory-bound academics – was a ludicrous failure.

Every organization generates efficiency by virtue of the mechanical order it promotes. Because of the incompatibility between the mechanical and the human, it also generates

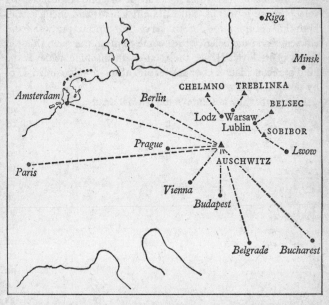

The pentagon of the death camps, Chelmno, Treblinka, Belsec, Sobibor and Auschwitz. Enclosed ghettoes are at Lodz, Warsaw and Lublin and in the general area inside the pentagon. To the east, unenclosed ghettoes occur in the Baltic States, as at Riga, in Russia, as at Minsk, in Eastern Poland, as at Lwow, causing privation and also feeding in to death camps. To the west and south, people from western and central European countries are brought in by train mainly to Auschwitz.

inefficiency, which can threaten to destroy the organization itself or crush the people it deals with. It is characteristic of the violent organization that, when threatened by its own inefficiencies, it tends not to reform them but to project them on to the people it deals with by becoming itself more violent. That is to say, violence becomes a substitute for efficiency and the organization crushes or kills more people than is necessary for its essential purposes.

But the total-death machine differs from other violent organizations in that it has no strategic or political purpose. Its sole purpose is to kill. Since its efficiencies and inefficiencies both kill people, they both serve its central purpose, and efficiency and inefficiency thus come to mean the same thing in terms of its logic. Hence the total-death machine achieves the kind of reconciliation of opposites and absolute value dreamed of by poets and philosophers.

Except that the absolute value is total death.

6

THE REST OF THE SECOND WORLD WAR, 1939–45

Toko in the Total Death Machine (11)

IN the last chapter I said that the sole purpose of the total death machine is to kill. Some might object to the application of this tag to the nuclear death machine. I have no wish to stand on theory in a matter where the realities are so obvious. However, the theoretical position is that no one has demonstrated convincingly that nuclear weapons can be used, in practice, in a controlled manner for strategic or political purposes. That is to say, the effects of the use of the weapons are unpredictable, and one of the major possibilities is that any human purpose in using them will be overwhelmed by the killing effects created by the weapons in operation; that the sole purpose will become, to kill. There are no probabilities in the situation, only possibilities. No general, whizz-kid or think-tank geisha can argue against this theoretical position. Not unless they are being paid at a specially high rate for their services.

How did we arrive at this dreamy logic?

Strangely enough, it has been inherent in the use of weapons throughout our century.

In a previous chapter I described the total-war machine as 'a machine of unpredictable event'. Again, those who sell their minds to the state or corporation cannot argue with this. There has never been any theoretical basis for a definition of total war. All we can do is describe the main features of total war the last time it happened.

From the example of the Second World War in Russia, the most intense on record, I have isolated four death-producing factors which may be used to measure the extent of a nation's involvement in total war. The nation may be, *First, a major theatre of military operations over a prolonged period:* ensuring the use of the most destructive weapons and technologies available, and their extension in space and time to produce deaths on scale. *Second, total-war methods – blitzkrieg, bombing, scorched earth – used against civilians as well as military:* providing a basic level of deaths from direct causes and from hardship. *Third, military occupation using arbitrary methods:* providing a basic level of executions, minor massacres, minor famines, major privations. *Fourth, the resistance of peoples:* producing, apart from prolongation of the war, deaths from partisan and underground activities, reprisals and counter-measures.

These factors brought twenty million deaths to the Russians. A similar spread of factors in China, a country where the population was twice as large and nearer to privation level, would have brought a much larger total. However, China was not a major military theatre in the sense of the weapons and technologies used, nor in the numbers engaged in actual combat. In the South, the amount of military combat was very limited. The initial military terror of the Japanese, in direct deaths and in the creation of refugees, and the prolonged occupation, produced a certain level of deaths. In North China the total-war methods used – the *three-all* policy of killing civilians and scorching the earth – initiated the process which brought the major volume of deaths. First, in the direct deaths and privations it caused. Secondly, it created a resistance in the people which brought about the swelling in numbers of the Communist armies, the intensifying and prolonging of combat activity, and hence further direct deaths and privations.

The ultimate significance of the resistance of the people in China was of course its contribution to the final victory over the Kuomintang and the establishment of the Communist state. As scholars have pointed out, the Chinese peasants did not resist for sentimental reasons. The pressures put upon them by the invaders were so intense that they had no choice but to join a force which gave them a chance of survival.

The *resistance of the people* thus has to be considered as a hard factor in total war. It is not necessarily marginal or sentimental. It varies according to the war situation and the type of population involved. The more it becomes a hard factor the more it becomes, like the other parts of the total-war machine, unpredictable in its effects. The implications of these points are fairly obvious. First, the resistance of the people has to be thought about most delicately in relation to reality, not sentiment. Secondly, despite Maoist doctrine there is no theoretical formula by which the resistance of the people can be successfully provoked, unless you count success in numbers of deaths. In China the resistance of the people was provoked by a massive accident of war. It became successful, in purposive terms, only after fifteen million people had lost their lives.

Apart from the Russians, twenty million, the Chinese, fifteen million, and the Jews, five million, the rest of the deaths in the Second World War numbered about fifteen million.

In assigning these fifteen million deaths to the nations that suffered them, I have graded the nations in the degree of their involvement in total war, according to the level of deaths and according to the four factors of total war mentioned above. I wonder what the reader will think of this theoretical classification.

Category I: Near-total involvement: Millions of deaths

	Number of deaths
Germany	5,000,000
Poland (excluding Jewish citizens)	3,000,000
Japan	2,500,000
Yugoslavia	1,700,000
Total	12,000,000 *approximately*

Although for some German citizens of great courage their country had been occupied since 1933, there was no intrusion of foreigners on her soil until the final stages of the war. Thus her home armies were not subject to wholesale capture and starvation, as the Russians were. Her civilian people did not die over prolonged periods of attrition, nor were they massacred and executed in large numbers. Most of the total-war activity of Germany was projected outwards from Germany. Hence most of the deaths were military. Up to the beginning of 1945 German military deaths were two million. In the last six months of the war about another half million died, and between one and one and a half million prisoners of war were sent to Russian labour camps where they are presumed to have died. Also in that period two million Germans fled from their homes and are unaccounted for; I have presumed that half a million of these may have died from various privations. Another half a million civilians died in bombing raids. Thus in the final period of the war Germany was subjected to a smaller version of the population movements and total-war methods that had occurred in Russia for four years. Those who died in air-raids were victims of a British total-war method, the terror-bombing of German cities, the best-known of which is the incineration and destruction of Dresden. This is said to have stiffened the resistance of the German people, though only to endure further in the trap of Nazism. The unpredicted result of the total-war machine for Germany was of course the division of Germany into two countries, not to mention the Communist takeover of the whole of Eastern Europe.

Poland was a major theatre of military operations for two short and devastating periods. The first was the original blitzkrieg attack of the Second World War, which Poland suffered in 1939; at the same time the Russians attacked Poland at the other end and carried off a million prisoners of war to the labour camps. The second was in the final period of the war when the Russian armies were pushing the Germans back across Poland; at the same time as this the Polish resistance movement in Warsaw rose up against the Germans. In all of these operations several hundred thousand Polish soldiers and partisans were killed, and a quarter of a million Polish prisoners are estimated to have died in the Russian labour camps. The major volume of Polish deaths came during the occupation period, from the privations of civilians in their homes and of soldiers and civilians in German camps. Of all countries Poland was the most abjectly crushed by military occupation, as well as being the site of the death camps. Including the Polish Jews, total deaths in Poland were in the region of five million, out of a total population of thirty-five million. In Poland the death camps are still preserved as monuments.

Japanese deaths in the war were two and a half million, including over half a million civilians. Of these, two or three hundred thousand were killed in U.S. bombing raids, including the atomic bombs dropped on Hiroshima and Nagasaki. This represents the only total-war method used against Japan outside of normal military operations. Considering the comparative figures of U.S. dead in the Pacific war, the major theatre of Japanese military operations, the total of nearly two million Japanese military deaths is very high. This is partly explained by the ratio of dead to wounded. In the American and British armies there were five or six wounded for every man killed. In the Japanese army twenty men were *killed* for every one wounded. The Japanese soldier was too fanatical to get wounded. He went the whole hog. If we remember that the Japanese total-war involvement, like the German, was mainly prosecuted against others, and in particular against Chinese peasants, an interesting comparison becomes clear.

The German repertory of total-war methods – blitzkrieg, occupation pressures on populations, burning crops, blowing up houses, reprisal massacres, political executions, starving and shooting of prisoners, death-camp technologies – was rationalized in the structure of those who carried out these operations. There was the ordinary German soldier; the crack Panzer soldier; the fanatical death's-head battalion trooper; the destruction squad and the massacre commando; the occupation administrator and the occupation thug; the SS trooper, the SS policeman, the SS camp guard. The Japanese had no such genteel rationale of destruction. When they sat on the peasants every soldier raped his share. When they burned, killed and looted every junior commander read the orders, every soldier did his duty. Of all the armies, only in the Japanese was the spirit of total war fully internalized in every soldier. It was a spiritual acceptance. They killed themselves as well as everyone else.

Yugoslavia was the country that refused to be occupied. In this case the resistance of the people was near-total. More than a million and a half deaths represents for Yugoslavia over one tenth of the population. Once again the German total-war machine forced Communism on Yugoslavia as it had made it inevitable in East Germany and Eastern Europe, and as the Japanese had made Communism inevitable in China.

Category 2: Major involvement: Half a million deaths

	Number of deaths	
France	570,000	
Britain and Commonwealth	460,000	
Italy	450,000	
United States	400,000	
Greece	360,000	
Rumania	350,000	
Total	2,500,000	*approximately*

Like Poland, France was a theatre of major military operations for two periods, one in 1940 and the other in 1944. Military deaths were almost two hundred thousand. The majority of deaths were due to occupation and the resistance of the people. Nearly half a million French civilians were killed by execution and by the privations of concentration camps in Germany. The French Resistance defines the second classic mode of resistance of the people as evoked by the Second World War. The first type of resistance, as it happened in China, Yugoslavia and Russia, was a massive resistance of the people organized in the ideological structures of Communism and expressing itself in military and para-military operations: an overt resistance. The French Resistance was under cover. It too was influenced by certain ideological structures but these were not essential to its organization. The structure of the French Resistance was basically the ability to organize inherent in large numbers of people in any advanced country. It preserved a shadow system of power, and of civilized values, alternative to the ethos of the occupying power and strategically essential to the free opponents of that ethos.

In Britain about a hundred thousand civilians died in bombing raids from Germany. This was the nearest the British came to suffering the effects of total war.

In Italy, a major theatre of military operations for part of the war, three hundred thousand civilians lost their lives, mainly through the devastation of towns and cities and the subsequent privations.

In Greece, the pressures of occupation and resistance brought a quarter of a million deaths from famine; fifty thousand civilians were shot by the occupying power.

In the United States such deaths were unknown, since America was not a scene of combat, nor of occupation, nor within reach of enemy bombers.

Category 3: Serious involvement: About a hundred thousand deaths

		Number of deaths	
Czechoslovakia		160,000	
Netherlands		145,000	
Hungary		100,000	
	Total	400,000	approximately

Category 4: Minor involvement: About ten thousand deaths

		Number of deaths	
Norway		10,000	
Bulgaria		10,000	
Belgium		10,000	
Denmark		5,000	
	Total	35,000	approximately

A Belgian would not thank you for suggesting that his country's involvement in the Second World War was 'minor'.

Occupation for five years by a foreign power has never been reported as a small matter. Norway, a hotbed of resistance during the war, would not consider its involvement trivial. Come to think of it, if you look at the Netherlands record – military 5,000 deaths, famine 15,000, bombing and shelling 20,000, concentration and labour camps 50,000, privation 50,000; if you consider that the Dutch brought many of these deaths upon themselves by acts of decency and courage in resistance; if you consider further that the Dutch made strenuous efforts to save the Jews in their country and that nevertheless a hundred thousand Dutch Jews were done to death ... then the involvement of the Netherlands appears as something more than 'serious'. As for Czechoslovakia, a country torn apart before the world war proper even began ...

In fact, the reality of what happened in these countries makes our system of classification look a bit silly. Yet none of them was involved in the full operative effects of the total-war machine.

There is a strange tangle at work here. Americans and British were in some sense more involved in the production of the total-war machine than any other countries. American soldiers were involved in some of the bitterest combat of the war. Their operations were conducted on a massive scale. In Britain, shortages, austerity, for some the constant fear of air-raids, depressed the whole level of national life. The more you think about it, the more ludicrous it becomes to minimize the part played by the people of these countries. Yet the full machinery of total war – military operations in the homeland, total-war methods, military occupation, the resistance of the people – hardly touched them.

Only in Britain and America – and, by a severe bending of the mind, in Germany and Japan – is it possible to preserve the myth that total war brings a majority of military and a margin of civilian deaths. The reality of total war is quite different. Of the fifty-five million people who died in the Second World War, about twenty million were soldiers, and of these at least five million died of starvation, disease and other causes in captivity. That is to say, two-thirds of the deaths were civilian, one-third soldiers, and about one quarter or twenty-five per cent of the whole were soldiers killed in combat.

Only in Britain and America – and, by a frantic inertia of the imagination, in Germany and Japan – is it possible to preserve the myth that the chief effect of total war is politically neutral technological advance. In reality, the major effects of total war, apart from the deaths, were: in France and Greece, civil war followed by many years of political instability; Communist takeovers in Yugoslavia, East Germany, Poland, Czechoslovakia Hungary, Rumania, Bulgaria – and in China, the largest nation on earth. Some technology. Some neutrality.

If national consciousness of the past leads to the conclusion that total war is an acceptable or desirable adventure for the future, then clearly there is something distinctly queasy about national consciousness. At the same time, the desire to see the dead in terms of the living culture of the present is a good, or at least a necessary, desire. It is the instinct to let the dead bury the dead. But supposing this good instinct leads to a forgetting of the past, so that the past repeats itself and leads to an unconscious pattern of thought whereby the dead threaten to bury the living? There we have a case where the instinct is good but the pattern of thought is unwittingly morbid.

I have hinted that Britain and America, because of their limited experience of total war, may be prone to such unconscious morbidities; and that in Germany and Japan, where the balance of aggression over suffering was so great, there may be a peculiar blindness on the question of total war. That such tendencies are true of many individuals in these countries there is no doubt. Nevertheless, to measure national attitudes to total war purely in terms of the volume of deaths suffered in the past is far from realistic. In the first place, it is absurd to suggest that a nation should mourn or honour its own dead in terms relative to the experience of other countries. A dead American or British soldier is likely to have suffered the same as a dead Russian. A Japanese boy killed in an air-raid went through the same experience as a boy killed in Warsaw or Shanghai or Coventry or Dresden or Stalingrad or Amsterdam. Furthermore, from what we know of national consciousness, and indeed from recent evidence, the chauvinism of Russia and of China may threaten to become strong enough to obscure their consciousness of their own major sufferings in the past.

How are we to resolve these contradictions and paradoxes?

I think we have to consider total war in terms of itself, and not in terms of particular national experience of it.

The total-war machine creates environments of differing intensity. The broadest and least intense of these might be called the survival environment. The people of a nation at total war are dedicated to the survival of the nation (or of themselves, if that is the direction of their efforts). They work for the war effort, they are subject to shortages, sacrifices, arbitrary mobilization. The survival atmosphere does not cover every corner of the country, but it covers most of it. It may be the atmosphere even of an occupied country. The citizen is aware of the broad threat to his environment from defeat or invasion or harsher administrative measures; and the remoter personal threat from air-raids or military occupation. Violent death intrudes into this environment to some extent; but the vast majority of people survive.

The second type of environment pertains in general battle areas, in areas where military occupation presses harshly upon the people, where there is partisan fighting and reprisals, and in cities under siege or constant threat of air-raids. This is the random-death environment: again, a majority of the people survive.

The survival environment and the random-death environment are imposed inevitably or 'objectively' upon people by the existence of total war and the presence of the total-war machine. The consciousness of total war which remains in the culture or society after the war is over is essentially a survival-consciousness.

The third type of environment is the environment of total death. We must look at this in the first place in subjective terms. The dying individual is surrounded by an immediate environment in which nearly everyone else dies as well. I hasten to add that I do not define 'total death' as a circumstance whereby every single human being loses his life. Only an idealist would make such a demand upon the resources of language. I take 'total death' to mean a circumstance in which the balance of death over life is well established. In this sense it is clear that war creates pockets of total death, and total war has a tendency to multiply the pockets of total death. These occur at the heart of the battle, in the most intense areas of the siege and the air-raid, in the famine or epidemic induced by occupation, in the villages where all inhabitants are killed as reprisal. I call these 'subjective' pockets because they do not exist as themselves, but as the intensest effects of a machine wider and more diffuse in its general effects. The eye of the storm only exists by virtue of the storm. It is the multiplicity of the pockets that aggregates the numbers of dead to enormity. But each pocket, because it is a phenomenon of intensity, is limited in its scope of enlargement. Among the largest pockets of total death were those German prisoner-of-war camps in which all or nearly all the Russian prisoners died. But these were still in a sense accidents in the evolution of the total-war machine.

The total-death environment only becomes 'objective', only achieves the ability to spread itself over a wide area, when there is a machine which exists for that very purpose. We have already seen one example of such a machine, by which an environment of total death was created for the Jews of Europe, an environment in which five million people died.

Now, survivors of the total-death environment (subjective or objective) are by definition few in number. Hence they do not embody, in the post-war society, a widespread consciousness of that environment. They do create an impact, but it is intense and specialized. The central consciousness of total war is based on experience of the survival and random-death environments. It is, very heavily, a survival-consciousness. However, since the chief effect of total war, distinguishing it from limited warfare, is the proliferation of pockets of total death and the creation of total-death machines, then the most significant experience of total war is that of the total-death environment.

I conclude that the reality of total war can only be apprehended, not by survival-consciousness but, if the reader will bear with me, by a consciousness of death.

I say 'bear with me' at this point because, having introduced the idea of death-consciousness, I do not at present have the means of making the notion any more explicit than the phrase itself suggests. I can however mention a few things which this particular death-consciousness does *not* resemble. It is not, I think, the same as death-wish, immediate fear of death, the death-trauma of wound or illness, morbidity, obsession with death, the poetic emotion of death, nor the aesthetic trauma of reading or seeing representations of horrible deaths. Most expressions of death-consciousness are intense and personal. But I suspect that the death-consciousness proper to the understanding of total war, and of man-made death in general, is not especially intense. It is something that will seem perfectly natural to all men a hundred years from now. Illustrating my feeling (it is only a feeling) that the coming and inevitable death-consciousness will not be intense, I have in my mind a picture of those few pious folk in the Middle Ages who made a practice of sleeping in their coffins. Now such a custom is not necessarily morbid or obsessional. Practised by a few people, it might well express a healthy respect for the fact of death. But if we all slept in our coffins, our culture as a whole would merely be obsessed with death. Death-consciousness in its intenser forms is not marketable in large quantities.

We should therefore learn to think of death without constriction of the breath, muscle tension, sudden headaches or backaches.

Consider, in relaxed fashion, the second form of the total death machine, the atom bombs that hit Nagasaki and Hiroshima in 1945. After all the painful evolution of the total-war machine, the gathering of pockets of total death in far-flung corners of the globe, the laborious and muddled development of the organizational total-death machine . . . here was a machine that could create an environment of total death over a wide area simply by the explosion of a bit of metal.

Strangely enough, the environment made by this political and scientific explosion was like the three total-war environments mentioned above, all in one package. Imagine a plate half a mile in diameter placed over the centre of the city. Ninety per cent of the people under the plate were killed. Extend the plate to one mile: in the further area, sixty per cent of the people were killed. I suppose that's your total-death environment. Moving outwards, it goes in controlled gradations of random death. One and a half miles, forty per cent deaths; two miles, twenty-five per cent deaths; two and a half miles, fifteen per cent deaths. Beyond three miles, the men women and children in their homes were allowed to survive, mainly. Some deaths, houses shaking or falling, little burns, radiation sickness. They were allowed to survive in that area because more scientific proofs were needed before total death could be spread at will.

I don't think you could properly call Toko a *citizen* of Hiroshima, since he was only eight years old. The status of children is theoretically always a difficult matter, but in practice it doesn't cause too much trouble because the parents are usually around to answer questions. Toko had that peculiar beauty which Westerners observe in Oriental children. Is that something real or is it something we invent in our fantasies? I suspect that in a sense we make it up. We are so used to regarding 'foreigners' in their political aspect, as caricatures of themselves, that when we are suddenly confronted with them in non-mythical form, that is as children, the shock is too much for us and we rave about their beauty, just as if we were talking about ourselves. Anyway, Toko had that common beauty, whatever its origin, that cannot entirely be explained by the way his close-cropped head rose at the back, or by his exceedingly black eyebrows or even by the dimply grin that split his face in two as he played in the streets of Hiroshima.

Now, everyone knows the circumstances in which that beauty was destroyed. But to explain the precise detail in the case of Toko raises a number of technical questions. Some people say that children have no separate identity from their parents. The child has no separate consciousness, he does not 'feel' things in the same way. Poor little mite, we say as we club him over the head or shoot him in an execution pit or drop a bomb on him – he doesn't understand what's going on. But his parents do. So long as we can consult the parents then we can determine the exact manner of his death, what he felt, how long it took and so on. But in the matter of killing children, unfortunately, and particularly in view of the modern scale of this activity, we do not always, or even usually, have the parents at hand. Therefore it is becoming increasingly necessary, for political, military and humanitarian purposes, to assign a separate identity to the child at war.

There have been many ingenious rationalizations of the killing of children. The best that has come to my notice, and one that should perhaps be put before the international courts for their consideration, is that one which was frequently used by soldiers during the Second World War, and is not unheard of today in the barrack-rooms of Viet-Nam. This is the argument that if the child is *not* killed he will grow up to be an enemy.

That is to say, since the child will grow up to be something unreal, he might as well be looked upon *now* as something unreal. That is the paranthropoid identity of the child.

7

OTHER TWENTIETH-CENTURY CONFLICTS

The Irregular

IT's our last chance to get the whole business of killing back on to a healthy basis. Imagine in the spanking dawn of our century a youth with dark fiery eyes, a lopsided tangle of curly hair awkward in its profusion, body and limbs ... still those of a mere stripling. But what experience was available to temper that growing strength! The Boer War, three long years of fighting at the cost of ten thousand lives: scene of the first concentration camps (the British), the first guerrilla warfare (the Boers). Can you doubt that our youth fought on the side of those doughty Boers in their struggle for freedom? The Boxer Uprising, scene of the first revolt against colonial influence, when foreigners were killed as a protest against their presence in China. I would have our growing boy steel his nerve in those massacres ... but there are technical difficulties. Instead, watch him become a man on the battlefields of the Russo-Japanese war, where the enormous guns were first used, precursors of the First World War. This was the first great killing of the century. It won the applause of the world. Japan became, in defiance of Kipling and geography, a typically Western 'power', honoured by all who revered the philosophy of grab. In the long course of time, in our own day, the Japanese even became 'white', while the Chinese remain 'coloured', in that land of sunshine and the freedom-loving Boers, South Africa. But here is the original score, from those far-off days:

	Number of deaths
1899–1902 South Africa: Boer War	10,000
1900 China: Boxer Rebellion	10,000
1902–4 Korea: Russo-Japanese War	100,000

In the remaining years of the decade our youth-become-a-man found himself in South America and Mexico where revolution was stirring. Always crisply got up, in the semi-military uniform that earns him the title *Irregular*, his broad clear brow rising to thick but well-trimmed curly black hair, a fringe of beard (covering, incidentally, a sabre scar inflicted by a Russian cavalryman), walking with a slightly bow-legged gait . . . the warm brown eyes of our hero never ceased to search for adventure and a cause to serve. In those early years, the Irregular had begun to compile a scrapbook of cuttings relating to the conflicts he had known, which he called *The Causes of the War*. Being a travelling man, he spent many relaxed hours leafing through this retrospective baedecker. *The Russians, seeking to extend their influence . . . The Boers, disturbed by increasing pressures . . . Rich deposits of coal and iron-ore . . . Naturally enough the Japanese, in their need for expansion . . . The discovery of gold brought people flocking . . . The British Government, on the other hand . . . Small bands of Chinese patriots . . .* On the sea-voyage from Mexico to Europe in the year 1911, the Irregular sipped at these phrases with considerable pleasure. He did not know what they meant, and they certainly did not relate to the experiences he had been through: but that was the pleasure. It was like having journeyed starving through Arctic blizzards for two months, having killed and eaten your companions and then, on reaching civilization, being rewarded with a good meal, a glass of hot toddy and a tale by the fireside.

The conflicts in which the Irregular now engaged had something to do with the break-up of the Turkish Empire in south-east Europe. First the Italians had a go at the Turks. Next year some of the Balkan states combined to attack Turkey. Next year the Balkan combination fought among themselves. Next year the Turks, now engaged against Russia in the First World War, had trouble with their Armenian subjects and began to deport and massacre Armenians on a very large scale.

For the Irregular, the experience was invaluable but in the end he had to get back to Mexico. This time, recuperating from wounds on the ocean voyage, he was more than ever reliant on his *Causes of the War. The Balkan League . . . The Turks, having only a small army in Europe . . .* He had partially lost sight of one eye through shell-blast, and it gave him a headache to read too much. *The Austro-Hungarian Empire, having divided by treaty . . . The Rumanians kept a watchful eye, hoping . . . Greeks, Bulgarians and Serbs combined . . .* The Irregular couldn't always read these lucid exposés through to the end, an attack of dysentery having left him with scarifying bowel movements. *However, the Italians felt the Turks were weak in North Africa . . .* His beard refused to grow on a large patch of dead skin on his left cheek, where the cut of a Bulgarian sabre was slowly healing. Only one thing in his new *Causes* really disturbed him, and that was the learned writers' use of the word 'atrocities' in relation to the Armenian massacres. The Irregular puzzled over this. Finally, he decided that those who provided him with hot toddy and fireside tales liked occasionally to have a look at what the travellers they entertained really got up to, and when they found out they called it an 'atrocity' and revelled for a brief moment in a fine anger. Rather like the gourmet who starves himself for a couple of days in order to rediscover the flavours of bread and cheese. It was the Irregular's first glimpse of the aesthetic view of killing. Nevertheless, he arrived back in Mexico as full of comfortable food and drink as troubled nature allows.

	Number of deaths
1911 North Africa: Italo-Turkish War	15,000
1912–13 South-east Europe: Balkan Wars	100,000
1914 Turkey: Armenian massacres	1,000,000

Mexico! in the second decade of our century was a paradise for a healthy, active man. 'Changes of government' were frequent. Civil war between revolutionary groups was common.

Foreign intervention (U.S.) was sporadic. Banditry was endemic. Peasants were dying. That was the Mexican revolution. Some say that a man in his thirties is at the prime of his life. The Irregular certainly flourished in this bracing atmosphere. Safe, warlike, decorated with military insignia yet retaining the casualness of civilian independence, smelling of warm bread and gun oil – the salt of the earth, really, the sort of man, you'd like to touch his cartridge-wrinkled tunic, just for luck. It was here that he perfected his technique of small-batch massacre – with the mounted machine-gun, with the lovely gatling-gun beloved of nine-year-old boys (*big* rat-tat-tat), with the rifle and even, given a squad of the proper heroes, with the pistol. Here also the Irregular developed certain small kindnesses, such as not shooting at peasants who had given him a bed for the night. A loyalty more warmly appreciated by some peasants than you might imagine. It's an old custom formalized in the Middle Ages when the feudal lord protected the lives of his own serfs and only killed other people's; surviving to this day in Sicily where the peasants still honour their lords and masters, the mafia; and come to think of it, not unknown in the Land of the Free itself.

	Number of deaths
1910–20 Mexican revolution and civil wars, including minor U.S. interventions (U.S.-Mexican Wars)	2,000,000

Every big war has its satellite wars, it seems, and the Irregular had business in Europe immediately after the First World War. Given the massive environment of weapons, destruction and conflict created by the world war and the Russian Civil War, we need only add the two well-known historical phrases: Russians and Poles, Greeks and Turks.

	Number of deaths
1919–21 Russo-Polish War	200,000
1919–22 Greco-Turkish War	500,000

Candidly, he had come to prefer the more free-ranging atmosphere of the North African deserts and of his beloved South America. There was always something going on in these parts. Since the withdrawal of *the Turkish presence* – as his *Causes of the War* put it – from the desert, there was *the British presence, the French presence, the Spanish presence.* Enough presence, really, to provide sort of long-term *causes of the war* so that the conflict itself in these parts was, as it was for the Irregular personally, a way of life. The bigger conflicts were just concentrated versions of what was going on all the time. And similarly in South America, where Paraguay and Bolivia were wrangling over the Chaco territory for some years, it was the conflict itself that came to matter. There were long spells of inactivity, necessary for the healing of those inevitable little wounds.

	Number of deaths
1919–25 Arabia: Nejd-Hejaz conflicts	30,000
1921 Morocco: Insurrection *v.* French and Spanish rule	30,000
1931 Iraq: Athurian rebellion	70,000
1928–35 Paraguay-Bolivia: Chaco War	500,000

During the 1930s there were ill-founded rumours that the Irregular had retired from the scene, or had succumbed to a fatal wound. Far from it! With unquenchable spirit, our veteran was conspicuous at the early triumphs of the New World Order of fascism. He assisted at the brilliant invasion of Manchuria, although owing to a temporary gonorrheal infection he was unable to join the Japanese in their celebration of that noble work. Despite a revisitation of the dysentery bug, he actually sat in an aeroplane – in the capacity of military observer – for a total of thirty-six hours during the Italian invasion of Abyssinia. The smell in the cockpit did not cloud his judgement in satisfying himself that the Abyssinian peasants were machine-gunned in accordance with the code of nations. As for the Spanish Civil War, and the illusions and betrayals of that conflict, the Irregular was in his element, for he did not know the meaning of either of these words. Our last flying glimpse of the Irregular, before the outbreak of the Second World War, is skating diplomatically – despite a broken leg and a steel plate in his skull – in the contest of arms between Russians and the mighty Finn. Certain Western governments needed sound evidence on which to base a possible switch of sympathies.

	Number of deaths
1931 Manchuria: Japanese invasion	300,000
1936 Abyssinia: Italian invasion	200,000
1936–9 Spanish Civil War	500,000
1939 Russo-Finnish War	200,000

With the beginning of the Second World War the Irregular – a specialist in 'small conflicts' – faced a well-deserved retirement. In wars and disturbances aggregating to an important total of over five million deaths, he had sacrificed half of his beard, the ease of one leg, half an eye, certain pieces of the skull and the comfort of regular bowel movements. He could browse happily through his *Causes of the War* with an undercurrent of realism which denied the validity of the *Causes* yet retained the pleasure of savouring their rolling phrases.

Nevertheless, when peace broke out in 1945 he was at it again. Now well into middle age, he was too grizzled in his ways to bother much about the ideological nature of the French and Greek Civil Wars. More familiar to him as a phenomenon at the heart of conflict was the British *presence* in Palestine and Burma, the Dutch *presence* in Indonesia.

	Number of deaths
1944–6 French Civil War	40,000
1945 Greek Civil War	50,000
1945–9 Palestine conflicts	20,000
1945–9 Indonesian Independence	30,000
1949–55 Burma Civil War	20,000

All the same the Irregular, in his efforts to earn a living, had to keep an eye on the way things were going. In that decade after

the Second World War, you could see the same patterns in both
the smaller and the larger conflicts. But if you looked at the large
ones separately a number of new and long-term developments
were clear. First, there was a determined effort to get rid of the
old *presences*, if necessary carried to the massive extent of the
independence war in French Indochina. Secondly, large-scale
internal disorders were possible in the *aftermath* of withdrawal,
such as the riots and killings which followed the British withdrawal from India and the partition of that country into India
and Pakistan (incidentally, a case of genuine demographic
violence). Thirdly, the internal presence of ideology in the new
state, and/or the external influence of existing Communist
states, constituted a *new presence*, as in the Korean War where
Chinese armies supported the North Koreans.

	Number of deaths
1946–54 Indochina Independence War	250,000
1947 Indian Partition disorders	1,000,000
1950–53 Korean War	1,000,000

There was thus developing in certain areas a general *environment* of arms, ideology and disorder, so that the Irregular's
Causes of the War was no longer a retrospective chapbook but
more of a guidebook to future events. In his seniority he was
often engaged in a consultant capacity and attended a large
number of briefing meetings before the outbreak of hostilities.
The notes he took were clipped into his *Causes of the War*. It
wasn't always easy to catch names at these hastily arranged
meetings, but the Irregular evolved a simple method of identification. *Economic Cause* tended to speak rather weightily but
with an impressive confidence in the obscurity of his arguments.
Military Cause was urbane and certain. *Ideological Cause* was
often a curious mixture of total conviction and random flippancy.
Sometimes more complex identifications had to be made such as
Socio-Economic Cause or *Geo-Political Cause*. The most difficult
to pin down was usually the leader of the group. This one
tended to keep a watchful, detached eye on the other *Causes* but
was himself characterized by more human attributes, such as

vanity, cunning, occasionally brutality but just as often sincerity or even passion. The Irregular watched for such signs until he was certain enough to note down his identity: *Chief Cause*.

The general environment of the late fifties continued to be one of withdrawal of old *presences*. The British, perhaps because they had *presences* in so many parts of the world that they were able to observe the coming pattern of events and respond to it, seemed to manage their withdrawals with smaller loss of life than some other states. And yet in Rhodesia they left a small enclave of white settlers who were prepared to suppress the people in order to maintain their own physical privileges. The Irregular noted this fact down in his *Causes of the War* for the future.

What the Irregular was looking for in the 1960s was a nice little environment of continuing violence that kept itself within suitable limits. Most of the new states, having rid themselves of *old presences*, were not particularly anxious to find themselves again dominated by *new presences* in the form of rigid ideologies. They preferred to develop themselves in the framework of the nation state, and from this circumstance a degree of state nationalism developed. If the orderly development of a modern state was threatened by outside ideologies, it could also be threatened internally by old tribal nationalism. Thus there were factional disturbances, in the Middle East among the Kurds and Sudanese, in India from the Naga tribesmen, in Kenya from the Somalis. These were contained within certain limits.

	Number of deaths
1960–64 India: Naga Rising	20,000
1962–4 Kurdish Rising	30,000
1965–7 Kenya: Somali Rising	6,000

The large, poor nations had sufficient mutual interest in national development not to let their border tensions, such as those between China and India, and India and Pakistan, get totally out of hand. Somewhat more threatening as conflicts were the Arab-Israeli war and the long-drawn-out deadlock between royalists and republicans in the Yemen.

	Number of deaths
1962–3 India-Pakistan clashes	7,000
1963–4 India-China clashes	5,000
1967 Arab-Israeli War	25,000
1962–70 Yemen Civil War	50,000

But these conflicts do not begin to express the nature of the 1960s. The large-scale deaths of the 1960s proceeded from conflicts grotesque in their development and exhibiting the characteristics of the most degenerate episodes of the Second World War. In a less grotesque era an old man like the Irregular would have been put out to pasture long ago. But thanks to the skills of technology he was still in a healthy condition. The threatened loss of his right eye, where a jagged splinter of shell casing had lodged, had been averted by an operation which lowered the socket area half an inch and the eyeball itself fractionally. The sores on his forehead – relic of a skin-graft which would not take – oozed pus of a freshness remarkable in a desiccating body. A youthful habit of picking at the scab that had once been his left ear (shell-blast) completed the pleasing liquefaction of his features. Dressed in crisp modern combat-kit, equipped with a Blatt-Philpott transistorized flamethrower, the Whibley-Bessier Mark IV (he would have none of the Mark III they offered him), and of course a high-repeating Cronier-Smith four-oh-shit ... well, he was just a dandy old fella. And just as dandy indeed were the Indonesian Civil War, in which a hundred thousand people were massacred for their ideology; the Viet-Nam War, in which a country of peasants was burned from the air; and the Nigerian Civil War, in which a million people were forced to starvation and death by a little conflict that began with a total of twenty thousand soldiers on both sides.

	Number of deaths
1966 Indonesian Civil War	100,000
1962–70 continuing ... Viet-Nam War	400,000
1967–9 Nigerian Civil War	1,000,000

Even the Irregular concluded that it might just not be possible to keep a nice little environment of violence going without it becoming bloody silly. He conceived a nostalgia for the old heroic conflicts of the past, and the old pioneering armies. He thought of the U.S. Cavalry of the nineteenth century. He thought of the tiny, desperate Red Army that defended Leningrad in 1917. He thought of the People's Liberation Army that roused the people in the hills of China in 1938. And he reflected that now, in this peacetime, the armed forces of these countries were standing at over three million men apiece. He thought of the honourable German and Japanese armies of the 1940s. Both had managed to destroy millions of people and still retain the idea of honour. But now you couldn't pick them out from their surroundings. In Europe excluding Russia there were four and a half million men permanently under arms. In Asia excluding China there were four and a half million men permanently under arms. Jesus Christ. He thought of the Holy Land, the Crusades, the warring sheikhs of the desert. Now in the Middle East there were half a million men permanently under arms. The world was manned by twenty million men professionally dedicated to violence.

He was getting a bit old (eighty-six). Were there no more strapping healthy deaths like in his youth? There were still small things going on in Africa, in South America. Perhaps there . . . There were guerrillas struggling for freedom in Angola, there were guerrillas struggling for freedom in Bolivia, in Guatemala, in Venezuela. There were guerrillas struggling with slot-machines in London, with professors in Paris. Guerrillas were trying to take over the Middle East. In New York female guerrillas were struggling with men.

It has been reported that the Irregular died a heroic death, but whether in Africa or South America, or with what other heroic guerrillas, I do not know. It is said that the manner of his death was a 'neat round hole' drilled in his forehead by a bullet . . . that from this neat round hole spurted fresh crimson blood . . . and that from this fresh blood the flower of freedom grew! I confess to a technical difficulty in imagining this scene. Consider the dilemma of an unfortunate man who is addicted to the dope heroin. He needs 'a fix', the needle in the vein. Quite simply, his arm is not amenable. It is shattered with fixes. He *knows* that just one more will settle everything, peace, happiness, economic miracles. But the veins in his arm deny further entry. They are hard, twisted, purple-knotted, dark as old shit. Yes, his living arm is as bleak as a park pavement where bourgeois ladies have walked their dogs.

I am as convinced as you, dear reader, that if we could just get a neat round hole drilled in the forehead of our Irregular, all else would immediately follow – poetic blood, freedom, flowers. But where, on the brow of that tattered old myth where the fresh pus spurts, should we find the very space for such a neat round fantasy?

8

THE UNRECONSTRUCTED
WORLD

Mohim in the Nature Machine

WHEN Mohim first came to Calcutta, to supply himself with the higher education, he was full of hope, and with good reason. He was the brightest boy for miles in his district; even the subsistence-level poverty of his family could not prevent him from shooting up to the university. He had imagined the tiny grant he had won in open competition would keep him going in Calcutta, but to his amazement his father had somehow found some extra money and pressed it upon him, with an air of great pride, on his departure.

Living was indeed hard, but Calcutta was so full of life, so colourful and exciting – and there were so many other students to share one's lot with. During his first couple of years Mo had a happy time. He gobbled up his studies, and it was this nourishment – not the vegetable curries and the occasional bit of meat and the constant rice – that made him grow a feeling of solidity and resilience within himself. His interest in politics had the same kind of firmness about it. He supported the Congress Party, and he could *feel* that the regime was right. It was democratic, it was tackling the immense problems of India: agricultural yield was improving, some headway was being made with birth control; the state was able to form capital for new industries and to exercise some control over the private sector; foreign capital did not shrink from participation.

Through eyes coloured by such readings in the newspapers Mo saw the poverty and wretchedness of the people of Calcutta. He was poor himself and could understand them. In one sense they merged into the traditional life of India, and you could not help but love India. With the love that he felt for his country – for its institutions, of which he was now part, and for the life of its people, from which he sprang – Mo knew with an inner certainty that the lot of even those living in the poorest part of the city, in conditions of indescribable filth and congestion, vulnerable to recurrent minor epidemics and to a constant toll of lives from malnutrition – must improve.

Must improve! that was the exultant fact. Already the average life expectancy of Indians was well ahead of that of nineteenth-century Europeans at the height of their industrial revolution. All the figures were improving – the infant mortality rate, the occurrence of famines and epidemics, the constant disease and malnutrition rate – all coming down. There was an inexorable logic of compassion in these social statistics which Mo took to himself. You could not cry over the past, nor could you immediately alter the massive rate, in the absolute sense, at which people were wasted away or struck down by uncontrollable nature. But you could bring the process under control, gradually. You could chip away at the waste and destruction of life, and each year the figures would be an improvement over last year's. Ultimately . . .

In his final year at the university Mo dabbled in Marxism. There were a number of reasons for this. On visits back to his village Mo was finding it increasingly difficult to mix in with his family on easy, natural terms. Sometimes he couldn't even remember how many of them there were. Including 'relatives' the tally was usually about fourteen, all living off a tiny patch of land. Not a great deal of work was done, but there was always a great cluster of people round the cooking pot when mealtimes arrived, excited, jabbering, self-congratulatory. The 'irrationality' of this system of living disturbed Mo profoundly. His comments upon it met with indifference or, although they were expressed in the most courteous manner, with crude rebuff. The arguments with his father were particularly soul-tearing for Mo, and he had to learn to hide his irritation with the old man's inability to understand any system but the one he was part of. What was gall to Mo was that his father by no means accepted the classification of 'ignorant', 'uneducated', 'backward' which Mo tolerantly bestowed upon him, but defended the status quo with vociferous tangles of prejudice, superstition and garbled chunks of the Vedanta.

At any rate, there was always back to Calcutta and the student crowd, and many of the brightest of these were Marxists. Their Marxism was often of an indeterminate sort, but their conversation was lively and full of satisfying certainties. 'Marxism is the only relevant thing the West has to offer us,' was one of the commonest of these. Some of the bolder spirits maintained an Anti-Americanism which Mo found heady but unable to adopt since he couldn't quite grasp the mystique of this attitude, although he listened fascinated to many expert analyses of the Anglo-Saxon temperament as being cold, aggressive/imperialistic and *instinctively uncivilized*, unlike the warm and *instinctively civilized* psyche of the continental European, Latin American, Russian and so forth. Some of his most hilarious moments were spent with such friends at the cinema, making fun of the audience's rapt and gasping reactions to the love- and war-torn passions of the Indian epic.

Mo really felt that he belonged to a new and insightful generation. He did not himself become an out-and-out Marxist, but his opinions changed through these contacts. For instance he came to realize that India's great problem was one of land more than of industrializing. This was such an obvious thought that he was ashamed to reveal to his friends that it had occurred to him as something new – and he assumed that to them it had always been obvious. They talked about the peasant problem and the difficulty of introducing new methods. Someone suggested that new techniques should be forced through. 'And what about those who don't agree?' – 'Send them to labour camps!' This was a high-spirited suggestion but it was taken up seriously and they discussed whether in all of India's closely cultivated area there was room for labour camps. Hill areas were suggested, and the edges of deserts, but it was finally agreed that the ideal kind of territory did not exist. 'Besides, our trains wouldn't be fast enough to get people there alive!' In the midst of the laughter someone excitedly insisted on the point. 'You don't have to move people physically. That's a crude application of science.' – 'What's the solution then?' – 'Thought control, like the Chinese use. You change people inside.' Mo thought about his father, his stubbornness and his mind full of old myths. – 'Impossible. You'd never do it. You might as well let them die in the trains!'

Another reason for Mo's leaning to Marxism was a growing sense of reality about the world he was about to enter. He still read the statistics of progress, but he couldn't help becoming aware, amid the intense gossip and stories of final-year students, that the people who were supposed to bring progress about – the people who ran the machine – did not live and work in the spirit of vigorous goodwill that had sustained him through his early university days. There was corruption in the machine, and apathy. Good people's ideas were frustrated, or, the struggle to get a place in the machine was so exhausting, the achievement such a triumph, that their vigour stopped there.

This was a problem more immediate than the grander ones Mo had read and thought about for the past years. He would soon have to face the problem of getting a job, in business or government. Students with the best marks usually got a place. Mo had unconsciously assumed he would be among these, but as his studies drew to a close the uncertainty became greater. On the last visit home before taking his final exams, he had a bitter quarrel with his father. Perhaps it was because of the under-lying fear of being unable to get a job, or perhaps because he had come home in a new mood of arrogance. He was full of the idea of 'industrializing agriculture'. This was the essence of the land problem, and the solution. It was quite novel to Mo, he imbibed it not as an idea that Marxists had had for fifty years but as a whole new way of looking at the land and the people upon it. Perhaps it was the final break with his own family, the final assumption of superiority. This would be his goal, in the career he hoped to find. But his father still looked upon him as a prize possession, one who was sure to do well in the exams and be a credit to everyone. This angered him, and they quarrelled.

Mo travelled back to Calcutta earlier than planned. In the train he had a confused mixture of emotions. Despite the quarrel and his vow to break with his family, his father had actually pressed money into his hand on parting, and said something which now kept ringing in his ears. 'The love of a parent for his child is the strongest thing in the world.' His father had said it sheepishly, as though ashamed of the emotion and trying to excuse the action of giving him money, and not expecting Mo to understand it. Yet it was the one thing his father had ever said that pierced his grown-up sensitivity. After years of superstitious sayings, old wives' tales, clichés, at last his father had said one sublime thing! And he understood it completely. In the flood of emotion for his father, he recalled another thing he had said. Mo had been talking about the need to mechanize agriculture, increase productivity so that fewer people would be needed to run the land. And his father had said bewilderedly, 'But where would we all go, if we were not all on the land? There would be hundreds of people wandering about the cities with nothing to do.' Mo had laughed hilariously at the old man's picture of the city. Hundreds! There would be millions! And this thought came back to him with a chill of fear, in the train. Already there were thousands in Calcutta with no jobs, and often no homes. Suppose an efficient agriculture made fifty, a hundred million people redundant, and industry quite unable to absorb them. Did the people running the country realize this? And then Mo felt foolish. Of course they must. Every time he had a new and blinding revelation, it turned out that the experts had known about it all along!

But it upturned all his new ideas about relations with his family, about Marxists and peasants . . . Everything was becoming confused. And in the surge of realism a final thought struck him. The money his father had given him, the sums he had given him over the past few years . . . where else could it have come from but money-lenders, charging back-breaking rates of interest? How on earth could they pay it back? There was only one way – they were relying on him, Mo, to find a big job with lots of money. And the exams were just two months ahead.

Mo did quite well in his examinations, but not brilliantly. Some of the best jobs were acquired by some of his Marxist friends. With their brilliance and wit they disappeared into the system. In the succeeding months, tramping from office to office looking for work, Mo came to accept their position without bitterness. It took them all their time to hang on to their jobs and make sense of the work they had to do, without trying to change or reform the system. Mo's first job was as messenger boy in a firm of city merchants, which he achieved by playing down his qualifications and looking at the same time energetic and submissive. After a few months the job was required for someone else. Mo understood, and left. For the first time he was left absolutely without money. The money from his father had long gone. He moved into a poorer quarter of the city where he payed a pitiful rent suitable to the wretchedness of the surroundings. Somehow he was able to live, mainly from a group of people he fell in with. Mostly ex-students like himself, they were out-and-out revolutionaries, short on theory and long on the desire for action. Viscerally, Mo agreed with their programme. Something had to be done. And they shared their rice.

When his revolutionary friends left to take part in some unspecified 'action' in the countryside, Mo had to find bits of work to keep him going. He could live cheaply enough, but he had developed a passion for films from the West. He should have saved his small surplus of money, but it all went on the cinema. What fascinated him about this cinema was not the glamour of the stars (Indian film stars were considerably more glamorous) but the way the people that thronged the streets in these films were well-dressed, casually healthy and apparently purposeful. It was a way of life more immediately comprehensible to him than his own life on the streets of Calcutta. Sometimes, coming out of the cinema, he was reassured about his own life; at other times the faces passing him on the street seemed dark and hopeless. Once he had the romantic notion of spending a week sleeping on the pavements, to find out what the people of Calcutta, the ones that suffered and lived the true weight of Calcutta, were really like. One night of that finished him. He slept, or tried to sleep, close to a group of beggars. They accepted him, in their circle of whining voices, grunts, throat-clearings and spittings, occasional wheezy laughs – but not in the way he'd imagined. They glanced at him without seeing him, grunted and whined at him whilst ignoring him, even spat and laughed in his direction as though he wasn't there. He couldn't sleep. He feared their knowledge of the night. Their stale and decomposing smells disgusted him. He was afraid of their hostility and afraid to show his own. Their chatter was entirely about pieces of food they had acquired, about whether one set of traffic lights was better to beg at than another, they talked incessantly about small sums of money but were afraid to mention the amounts they had begged. As soon as dawn was decently established, he fled back to his little room, and slept.

He saw in the newspapers that his revolutionary friends were killing landlords in the provinces, according to Maoist doctrine. In the cinema one day, along with the American film, there was a documentary about Calcutta. All around him were whispering, recognizing landmarks. But Mo was gripped by a face that kept recurring in the film. It was the face of an old man, hollowed with hunger, the eyes sunk in an intense, dark misery. Mo was ashamed that this should be India. For a moment he agreed with his killing friends. 'Anything! Anything!' his mind shouted in the dark of the cinema, 'so that this should be swept away!' And this sweeping away filled his head with a joyous vision.

In the real throng of people outside, Mo was disturbed by the thoughts he had had in the cinema. In an instant he had imagined that this variety of living faces, some absorbed, some listless, some wretched, should be 'swept away' and replaced by . . . by nice, clean, attentive, hygienic, well-fed faces! It was a false vision, but how had it ever managed to enter his mind? For he lived with these people, and even on that night with the beggars whom he heartily feared and hated, he had never for one moment imagined that they should not be allowed to live, that they should be 'swept away' simply because he could not bear to look at them and hated and feared being close to them. There must be an important difference, Mo concluded, between living with people and having fantasies about people.

Nevertheless Mo himself, although he had begun to discover some hard truths in that difficult area where fantasy is confronted by real life and real life by fantasy, was in the end unable to keep himself alive; there was no more work, and no more food, and the simple business of digestion and circulation of the blood and breathing had to come to a stop, and Mo died of starvation in a small room in Calcutta.

Book Two

ANALYSES:
PARTS OF THE
MACHINE

9

AGENTS OF DEATH

DEATH MACHINES

In considering violent or untimely death, it is the manner and means of death – not the general phenomenon of death itself – that are of primary philosophical interest.

Can the manner and means of violent death be reduced to a knowable mechanism – a 'death machine'?

Of the ways in which we can think of knowing or understanding such a death machine, one is to 'know all the facts', another is to ask the question, 'how does it relate to me?'

To know the facts is desirable. To know *all* the facts about such a phenomenon as the death machine would clearly be an absurd pretension. Yet, 'waiting for science to establish all the facts' is the everyday limbo of the game of factual knowledge. Whilst playing this waiting game we are supposed to suspend the judgement of values, and even to neglect that most sensitive tool of inquiry, sharpened by experience, alert to survive, vivid in its brief life: intuition. Intuition, or the practice of relating oneself to the object in the immediacy of experience, is, like life itself, 'unreliable'. It seems that the certainties of science are worth waiting for. But when these so-called certainties appear they are as pluralistic, as conflicting, as subject to opinion as anything else. In short, the procedures of 'objective' inquiry are just as much modified by self and by fantasy as those of subjective inquiry. The difference is that in the first case the part played by the self is concealed from the observer, and often from the would-be scientist himself.

Shelley said that the poet is the 'unacknowledged legislator' of the world. In our grim times the chief unacknowledged legislator has been the subjective fantasy of political leaders, academic theorists, social groups masquerading as 'objective reality', 'historical necessity', 'political realism', 'value-free judgement', 'scientific objectivity' and so forth.

The death machine, then, is partly a factual object – an ever-incomplete accretion of facts; and partly a philosophical object – uncertain of definition yet conceived as a whole to which I relate myself, so intuitively that the 'I' itself will become, if necessary, subject to analysis as part of the death machine!

We might manage a preliminary definition, or at least tease out some of the relevant parts, of the death machine if we look at those versions of it which I have already loosely identified with different areas of macro-violence. The *war machine*, the *total-war machine* and the *total-state machine* are pretty well factual objects, identifiable in terms of organization, weapons, production, deployment of plans and personnel.

I took the war machine of the First World War as the type of the twentieth-century war machine. What characterizes it most is a change in the nature of the *alienating process*. War was traditionally a conflict between two alienated sides, 'enemies'. During the First World War even the men in the trenches ceased to believe that the enemy was the men in the other trenches. The alienating process of the modern war machine divides men into two subjective environments: the physical environment of the victim (the death environment) and the technological environment of the systems and machines which produce death. Some have perceived this in terms of class alienation. According to this view, the killing systems and machines are within the conscious control of the leaders and generals, and it is their class alienation from the poor that prevents them from using restraint in the use of these systems against the chief victims, the ordinary soldiers who without their uniforms are, of course, the poor. I am sure that this process – which I shall call *natural alienation* when I discuss it below in the context of the nature machine – is relevant to a discussion of how the modern war machine came into being, or evolved. The other view is that the machines and systems inhabit a faceless

AGENTS OF DEATH

environment of their own, and dominate their users. However it
evolved in the first place, it is this, which we can fairly call
technological alienation, that remains and persists as the most
characteristic feature of the twentieth-century war machine.

It is also characteristic of the war machine that the same man,
the soldier, operates the killing systems as well as being their
victim. The *total-war* machine extends the alienation principle,
for here death environments are also created for people who are
not themselves involved in operating the killing systems, that is
civilians shot, starved or bombed, soldiers and civilians enclosed
in camps. Here the alienation between the environment of the
killing system – military or administrative – and the environment of the victim, is total. The same is true of the total-state
machine, with one additional refinement. The alienated identity
of the victim is not merely created by the technological sweep of
the machine, as it is in the total-war machine. In this case,
before the victim is included in the killing technology (the labour
camp, the mass execution, the deportation) a paranthropoid identity, such as class enemy or enemy of the people, is created for
him out of the ideology of the total-state machine. That is to
say, *ideological alienation* precedes the technological alienation.

The essential difference between the war machine and the
total-war machine is one of *consciousness*. Traditionally war was
a ritual in which certain qualities such as bravery, generalship,
morale, cunning contributed to the symbolic outcome known as
'victory'. Where ritual and symbol broke down you had
chaotic, meaningless conflicts such as the Thirty Years' War.
The First World War was *not* this chaotic, meaningless thing,
not merely the war of attrition and exhaustion. It was a case –
the case – of ritual and symbol being outstripped and replaced by
a new logic of war. But it was not yet a conscious logic. Total
war as it developed thereafter was a *conscious* departure from the
natural order provided by ritual and symbol. But how conscious?
and how true has the logic of the new order been to the human
consciousness?

As we know, the raw material of total war, and hence the chief
premises of its logic are, one, vast numbers of people and, two,
machines.

T.C.B.–7   119

The vast numbers were first represented by the figure of the citizen-soldier, who reached his apotheosis in the First World War. By the Second World War he was already outstripped, in numbers participating, by the plain *citizen*. The next total war will involve very few soldiers as against citizens. Thus the logic of numbers reaches its conclusion, that total war is war between citizens not soldiers. But this logic cannot sustain a theory of war. 'Soldiers' means a selective, limited number of people who can be used for purposive action. 'Citizens' has no such finite, purposive meaning. It can only mean either 'all citizens' or 'citizens at random to an infinite number'. It is an inchoate principle which cannot sustain a theory of conflict.

The responsibility for providing a rationale of total war thus devolves heavily upon the machines, and the logic of the machines is utterly fascinating. We should remember, first, that the machines of modern warfare are not merely horrid excrescences, nightmarish extrusions of the human mind. That is what they become in action, but purely as machines they are truly representative of us and the times we live in. The force of unprecedented numbers; impersonal answers to the demands of conflicting egos; the development of solutions under pressure; economical concentration of human ingenuity – all of these are represented and symbolized in our machines of warfare. They are our champions on the field of conflict.

It is part of the genius of living things that violence, when not directed to survival (food, protection), is economical in its effects. The biological response to conflict between equals is an instinctive ritual which (a) recognizes and respects the reality of the conflict or disagreement, and (b) reduces the struggle to symbolic dimensions. Animals fighting their own kind have a system of signals symbolizing defeat, victory, submission which allow the conflict to be resolved far short of irreparable physical harm. Human society is far too complex for such patterns to remain in a pure form, but they still survive at the roots of individual behaviour. So far as group conflict is concerned, the most economical fighting ritual is that where two champions symbolize two numerous groups of people and fight on their behalf.

When it comes to the *machine as champion*, not only does the machine lack these reductive qualities: its response to the conflict situation is purely quantitative. Where there are two machines confronting one another, there will be soon four, and so on. The symbol or champion becomes greater in importance than what it represents. As the number and power of the machines increases, so does the number of people involved. But as we have seen, the logic of numbers in the context of total war cannot sustain a rationale of conflict. Once again we reach a logical *impasse*. There is only one logical path left, and that is that the machines should fight one another *without the involvement of people*.

There are I think two possible reasons why we do not proceed with this logic and have a War of the Machines. One is the difficulty of arranging it; but I cannot believe this would be an insuperable obstacle. The other reason, and I believe the valid one, is that it would be absurd. For two opposing sides to contemplate arranging a War of the Machines would expose the absurdity of the logic of conflict by destructive machinery, and hence must lead to the dismantling of the machinery. But this is something that we could not bear to contemplate. So great is our spiritual and material investment in the machines, so much do they truly champion our values, so little do we have the wit or resourcefulness to devise other symbols to represent us in our conflicts, that we cannot face up to the logic of what we are doing. So the people and the machines continue to grow in numbers, the function of the people being to lend verisimilitude to the War of the Machines. Thus we achieve the poor man's version of sanity, which is the physical acceptance of whatever happens to exist, supported by whatever rationalization can be concocted at the moment.

I began by asking how true the logic of total war has been to the human consciousness. Well, it is a straightforward denial of consciousness, of course. If the machines are looked upon as the objective results of thought, and in their development as the repositories of an objective logic, then the objective conclusion they display is, as demonstrated above, the need for their own destruction or dismantling. Consciousness demands that we draw this conclusion and act upon it. Indeed, if looked upon in this way the machines of war might provide the basis for a complete rationale of the place of conflict in human society, and of the destruction of human life in particular. In this case they would perform a useful rationalizing function, and would actually take human practice a progressive step beyond the simple logic of survival which governs the instinctive rituals of fighting. But, in the denial of this consciousness, we leave ourselves in that limbo known as the world of objective reality: a world of external objects in which the human being has no greater value than any other object displacing the same physical volume of space, a mental environment as hostile to the survival of life as a concentration camp.

What is the difference between the 'nature machine' and these man-made death machines? Well, the *nature machine* is the mechanics of what used to be called, rather smugly, the balance of nature. It was a kind of long-term death machine for the poor in their environment, in the form of disease, epidemic and shortage of food; tendencies that were exacerbated from time to time by natural disasters such as flood and crop failure, and by degenerate relationships between alienated classes. But the balance of nature was kept in the sense that life triumphed conspicuously over death.

On the basis of this definition we can draw some comparisons between death in the natural environment and in the man-made environment. By 'natural environment' I mean the context of living when the world society as a whole was pre-industrial. Many of the same conditions apply to present-day 'under-developed' countries. But remember that however pre- or non-industrial a society may be today, it almost certainly possesses two basic ingredients of the man-made environment: modern medicine, which may drastically reduce the death-rate and increase the population; and, at the least, rapid access to sophisticated military technology in the world community. The essential elements of the new man-made life and death.

If we think of untimely deaths in the natural environment as being the 'violence of nature' then by far the greatest proportion came from *micro-violence*, by which I mean the regular, widely distributed incidence of disease, infant mortality, malnutrition. Because of the gradual, pervasive nature of micro-violence we tend to lack direct ways of apprehending its magnitude. For the same reason its impact is taken and absorbed by those directly affected by it: it does not *apparently* affect the structures of society as a whole. The macro-violence of nature – floods, famine, pestilence – had more apparent, dramatic impact, but in fact the quantitative effects were much smaller; and macro-violence was not institutionalized and given a continuous existence as it is in the man-made environment. The same was true of the macro-violent forms of fighting, which retained an inherent *reductive capacity*; whilst in the man-made environment, where the propensity to fight is invested in machines, the problem of reduction is divorced from instinct, ritual and commonsense and is a problem of men and machines, and which controls which.

The chief reason the effects of micro-violence are unapparent is because it is an essential *part* of the social structure. The 'balance of nature' depends upon it. So does the large-family structure and hence the specialized roles of men and women. Natural micro-violence has a macro-violent impact only when the possibility of stopping it is perceived – then it promotes change or revolution; and when it *has* been stopped – then it promotes (in default of birth control) a population explosion with future implications of macro-violence.

The alienation process in the natural environment has the same roots as in the man-made environment, but develops in a radically different way. *Natural alienation* begins as a good and necessary separation of vigorous social elements from their bondage to the earth. As this separation flowers into the skills and arts of social management the class formed from it, whether aristocratic or middle-class, become physically alienated not only from the earthier aspects of themselves but from the people associated with the earth; hence the despised class of *peasants*. In spite of this actual circumstance, of people living as it were in separate physical worlds, the Christian ethos claims to unite them. The people are spiritually united in God, and even physically united in a romanticized version of nature. When this unified consciousness is challenged or threatened we have *religious alienation*, the victims being, in the post-Reformation period *minority Christian* denominations, in the turbulent and insecure seventeenth century *witches*, and persistently throughout the Christian centuries the *Jews*.

Physical and spiritual alienation is thus, in the natural environment, natural and religious, and in the man-made environment, technological and ideological. The victims are similar and the relevant psychological patterns seem to be very much the same. Peasants and Jews are major victims of both types of environment; they are the link as it were between the paranthropoid identities of one kind of society and the other. The great difference is in the kind of violence they bring about. The natural environment contained a continual micro-violence which took a regular toll of human life and from time to time escalated sufficiently through plague, famine and the chaos of war to give society a nasty jolt, but it preserved the balance of nature and never at any time threatened the existence of the human species. The man-made environment has brought micro-violence impressively under control, but it threatens to disturb the balance of nature through industrial activity affecting the atmosphere, through the destruction of living species and through uncontrolled increases in human population; it has brought macro-violence to a level which disastrously upsets the stability of societies, destroys morale and threatens the continued existence of the human species.

Another link between the two environments is the *death-breeding machine* which at its most chaotic combines the violence of nature with that of technology. If technology is nature moulded by consciousness then we might expect this machine to contain a progression from a less-conscious to a more-conscious process. Certainly human consciousness is embedded in technology, yet apologists of modern war tend to present the technology as a massive simulation of nature about which little can be done; and it does seem more like a progression from blind nature to blind technology. If we extend the meaning of the *death-breeding process* to signify the active principle of all macro-violent systems, we shall see however that some are more conscious than others. Also we should remember that technology proceeds from a knowable first cause: man or, more specifically, scientific man. The death-breeding process leads to the final peak of the *total-death machine*, that which threatens the apocalyptic end and absolutely final appearance of . . . us.

What about . . . us? the celluloid lovers continually ask each other as we catch our breaths in the dark of the cinema, and that is also the question of the total-death machine. I suppose total death is some kind of absolute value and the philosophical core of the man-made death machine. Looking at the death machine as a philosophical entity, we might see the *nature machine* as the basic source of all; the *death-breeding process* as the active principle with its question about consciousness; and *total death* as the final question.

In the natural environment nature is supposed to unite society in happy worship of God. In the man-made environment technology is supposed to unite society in happy worship of Science. But if we look at the technologies of macro-violence we shall soon see that the reality is very different.

TECHNOLOGIES OF MACRO-VIOLENCE

Of the 110 million man-made deaths calculated in this century, sixty-two million died in conditions of *privation*, forty-six million from guns and bombs, or *hardware*, and two million from *chemicals*. In separating out *chemicals* as a category on its own I am thinking of the future as well as reflecting the century's progress from the heavy metal industries to the advances in the chemical industries which are such a significant part of our present-day scene. The familiar association of large-scale killing with factory production is not merely a colourful metaphor. Given the scale of modern killing technologies, their parallel development with that of industrial research and methods is inevitable. Hence the latest developments in killing methods are those associated with the fashionable science of the moment, biology.

Privation Technologies

The basic kinds of privation technologies are I think best expressed as operating in *enclosed, semi-enclosed* and *diffuse* areas.

Deaths from privation technologies 62 million		
ENCLOSED	SEMI-ENCLOSED	DIFFUSE
Camp privation	City privation	Rural or mixed privation
20 million	16 million	26 million

Enclosed Privation Areas

Camp privation is a highly conscious process, involving collection and movement of people, and selective identity of the victim. The systems of the killing technology are various: camp administration, collection or concentration system, and the wider governmental system directing all. Where the secret police system is a power in the land these functions are vertically integrated. But the people who perform the different functions, even if belonging to the same organization, differ from one another, partly in class and outlook, certainly in their spatial relationship with the victim. Where there is no curb on the

ENCLOSED PRIVATION AREAS

Camp privation

Enclosed ghetto, 1 m. deaths

Concentration camp, 2.5 m. deaths

Prisoners-of-war camp, 4.5 m. deaths

Labour camp, 12 m. deaths

power of the state (the first condition for camp privation), the state's victims are passed on *notionally* by those who make the rules, *administratively* by those who run the identification and collection system and *physically* by the camp administration and guards. They are delivered from one set of people to the next. Arbitrary brutality occurs in those who are brutal by nature. But when the conditions notionally or administratively laid down are inhuman, and are supervised by the kind of people who survive by obeying orders, then the system is brutal and that is a more powerful force than arbitrary brutality. The most powerful force of all is physical neglect.

The *enclosed ghettoes* of Poland – Warsaw, Lodz, Lublin – were used as camps. They were sealed-off city areas into which people from outside were concentrated. They were virtually total-death environments. They are unique as enclosed privation areas in which the identity of the victim was not selective as to age and sex (although it is true that less severe privations have been suffered by entire families in transit camps for deported populations and in displaced person camps for refugees).

The German *prisoner-of-war camps* for Russians were the only enclosed privation areas with entirely male populations. Some of these camps were certainly places of total death. They are the most extreme example of sheer physical neglect, more powerful in its effects (cannibalism, for instance) than enforced human pressures.

Although the degeneration of conditions in the German *concentration camps* was possibly due to the secret police arm in particular, the German camps as a whole reflected the policy of the government over a period and hence to a very large extent the society as a whole. Racist attitudes were responsible for the ghettoes, and for the treatment of Slav prisoners-of-war in a way different from people of other races. The German camp system in its developed form was possible only as the result of military conquest, and with military co-operation. Nine-tenths of the victims were foreigners. Any individual actions leading to their presence in the camps were committed in response to military aggression. In the chain of people who pass on victims from one to the other, the military acted as delivery men to the secret police, not only in the case of some of the concentration camp victims, but also in the case of the Russian prisoners-of-war.

Whilst the German camp system lasted little more than the duration of the war, the Russian *labour camps* have the distinction of being a permanent assertion of a national system of injustice, traditional in its present form for over fifty years. This is the only camp system where privation has been imposed on people for more than about five years. Hence the environments created by the system – virtually a conscious re-creation of the micro-violence of nature – are unique. Within the system, all on a large scale, are a survival environment, a random-death environment, and a total-death environment. There are certain special camps where people are deprived of liberty but otherwise not harassed. These are the camps of the survival environment, which Solzhenitsyn's novel describes as *The First Circle*. Beyond this there is the second circle, of the labour camp proper and the random-death environment. Beyond that there is the third circle, the camps of the far North and East and the total-death environment: Komi, Karaganda, Vorkuta.

Semi-enclosed Privation Areas

Privation technologies in semi-enclosed areas emphasize the vulnerability of cities. A city cannot adapt itself to military strategies. It cannot pretend it is not a city, disguise itself as a forest, grow its own food on the sly, and so on. Its citizens depend upon organizational structures and if these are inter-

SEMI-ENCLOSED PRIVATION AREAS

City privation

Unenclosed ghetto, 1 m. deaths

Siege, 1 m. deaths

Occupation, 6 m. deaths

Civil dislocation, 8 m. deaths

fered with so is the life of the citizen. Once disruption gets beyond a certain stage there is nothing much that can be done about it. Total war and total revolution bring the random-death environment to the city.

The *unenclosed ghettoes* of Eastern Poland and the Baltic States were subject to harassment and pressures from the occupying forces, for racialist reasons, which turned them into total-death environments. The purely military pressures of *siege* almost did the same for Leningrad. On a larger and somewhat more diffuse scale, the cities of Russia became areas of random death from privation during the *dislocation* of the Civil War period and again under the pressures of military *occupation* during the Second World War.

The victims of city privation are of course families in their normal habitats; in time of war their identities are selective to the extent that the younger men are being killed elsewhere.

Diffuse Privation Areas

It's amazing in how many different ways the life can be squeezed out of people. It had never occurred to me that a sizeable number of people might have died in *transit* – in the

DIFFUSE PRIVATION AREAS

Rural or mixed privation

Combat, 1 m. deaths

Transit, 1.5 m. deaths

Economic blockade, 2 m. deaths

Man-made famine, 5 m. deaths

Scorched earth, 5 m. deaths

War dislocation, 12 m. deaths

sheer bungling inefficiency of forced movement. Think of the way human beings have been driven and herded back and forth across Europe and Russia in our century. Deportation of peasants to Siberia. Trains to the labour camps. Deportation of Russian and Ukrainian slave labourers to Germany. Trains from every corner of Europe to the ghettoes and death camps. Rail journeys and forced marches of prisoners of war.

Privation deaths among soldiers in *combat* conditions include the typhus and wound infections of the First World War, the freezing hardship and disease of the Second World War in Russia, the starvation and typhus of the China War and amongst other ill-equipped armies throughout the century, the malarias and jaundices of Western soldiers in the East.

You would imagine that *diffuse* privation would have a larger element of the accidental about it, if only because of the sheer difficulty of getting at people in far-flung rural areas. But not so. *Economic blockade*, as practised against the Germans in the First World War, against the Biafrans in the Nigerian Civil War; *man-made famine*, as engineered against the Russian peasants during the collectivization; *scorched-earth* tactics, as used by the Germans in Russia and the Japanese in China. They are all highly conscious and deliberate methods of destroying people: killing technologies.

Most of these highly conscious technologies tend to produce an immediate random-death environment. In the case of the general *war dislocation* in China and other places where a slow privation was diffused over a vast population, you might say that the privation deaths were an intrusion into a survival environment, that is to say a social climate in which death is not random but people still have some room to survive by their own efforts.

Listing these technologies, as objective parts of the death machine, is not difficult. But how can I, as an individual, relate myself to these? Perhaps we all tend to feel we ought to attempt to re-live the sufferings of the dead. Apart from the self-delusion involved in such an attempt, it is difficult to see what object is served by it. It certainly doesn't bring back the dead or heal their agony or expiate the crimes of which they are the victims.

In fact, if you read some of the basic factual accounts of the intensest death environments such as concentration or death camps – as you must do, if you hope to reach any understanding of the human story – you will probably have an *involuntary* 're-living' of suffering in any case. The experience of most people I have talked to on this subject agrees with my own – that the simple factual detail of such accounts is so horrifying that it is only bearable for a few pages at a time. Herein I think lies the salutory and sole purpose of 're-living' such sufferings: the perception of the unbearable. If it is bearable something phoney is going on, either on the part of the writer or of the reader.

I cannot then truly relate myself to these technologies of macro-violence through the simulated emotions, feelings and sufferings of the flesh known as 're-living.' But I *can* suffer these structures of reality – these terms descriptive of real event – to enter the mind undistorted by specific colour, myth or image.

Indeed it would be difficult enough to describe the *ghetto*, the *blockade*, the *scorched earth*, the *famine*, in terms of image or metaphor – for these are the basic realities which provide image and metaphor for the rest of ordinary existence. They are the bare bones of reality. Nor is there much need, in order to convey their reality, to explain in great detail how the *siege* or *occupation* come into being and work their effects, for the bones of death are easily enough achieved. There is nothing extraordinary about any of these – they could be organized by a wise child if there were a wise child willing to organize millions of deaths. If we were describing some complex social fabric where a million conflicting interests were maintained in a living pattern then there would be some call for depth of study ... but when it comes to the *prison camp*, the *concentration camp*, the *labour camp*, all of these share that cretinous unity of human purpose whereby success and failure achieve the same end of destruction and death. These are the bones, these technologies of the past and those death systems latent in our present, that form the skeleton structure of the death machine.

If it is true that in the twentieth century man has finally come face to face with his own skeleton, it is a structure such as this that he is looking at. I would have the *intellect*, not simulated feelings but the perceiving *mind*, suffer that skeleton.

Hardware Technologies

Military experts tend to assert that in twentieth-century conflicts many more deaths have been caused by the big guns than by small arms. In this generalization there is an important truth and an important untruth. Quantitatively, the statement is not true. According to my calculations deaths from hardware technologies divide roughly as follows:

Deaths from hardware technologies 46 million			
BIG GUNS	AERIAL BOMBS	SMALL-ARMS	DEMOGRAPHIC (mixed)
18 million	1 million	24 million	3 million

But the *significant* untruth lies in the implication that as deaths from the big guns increase, deaths from small arms might, or do, or by some logic should, decline in numbers. Not only is this a demonstrably false proposition, but it is the very opposite that is true. As deaths from big guns increase, they also help to bring about an *increase* in deaths from small arms. This is the important truth about the death-potential of the big guns. It is not a question of a particular type of weapon being chosen for military reasons, or of one type making another type obsolete. It is a question of big guns *creating an environment* of death on the scale of macro-violence. In this environment small arms and other death technologies not only flourish but also tend to increase to the same scale of macro-violence.

Big Guns

Basing itself on the general nature of the First World War and on some evidence suggesting the preponderance of wounds to be from the effects of exploding shells, expert opinion concludes that 'ninety per cent' or 'three-quarters' of the deaths came from the big guns. We may modify that proportion if we assume that experts tend to think exclusively in terms of combat deaths, chiefly in terms of the major theatres of war and mainly of the most characteristic set-piece battles. On the basis of a ten million total, at least two million deaths (from the economic blockade and from soldier-disease) were outside of combat. If we think of the early part of the war when the machine-gun was used intensively, of the massed cavalry charges of the Russian front and the heavy losses on the Italo-Austrian front, as well as continuous small engagements and sniping throughout the war, it becomes at least possible that as many as three million may have died from small-arms fire.

BIG GUNS

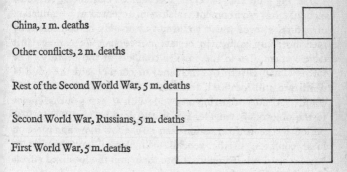

China, 1 m. deaths

Other conflicts, 2 m. deaths

Rest of the Second World War, 5 m. deaths

Second World War, Russians, 5 m. deaths

First World War, 5 m. deaths

Even if the proportion of deaths from the big guns was as low as five million out of ten, the experts are certainly correct in emphasizing the overwhelming significance of these weapons. The big guns created a physical and mental environment, a list of whose effects on the human race would break the spirit of any computer. The mechanical scale of the big guns determined strategy and the general context in which twentieth-century conflict would take place. The big guns decided that the characteristic form of killing in the twentieth century would be repetitive massacre, with a minimum of felt conflict. Thus the nature of the *small-arms* killings in the First World War was predetermined by the big guns. In the first place, whether they amounted to one or three million, the number was greater than the number killed by small arms in any previous war. Secondly, probably the majority took the form of repetitive massacre in situations created by the logic of the big guns.

In the First World War the big guns were heavier and the distinction between them and small arms was cruder than in the Second World War. Rifles and machine-guns – dominated, like the minds of generals, by the big guns – did the work of the big guns. That is to say, they were frequently used for massacre in situations where big guns might as well have been used. In the Second World War big guns were generally lighter and the range of weapons wider. Some were even portable. Weapons had been rationalized to meet the techniques of massacre.

The big guns and, later, the mechanized battlefield, created a technological environment which men accepted as a simulation of nature, a force which could not ultimately be controlled by men but only guided in certain directions. We can see this development also in the smaller conflicts of the century. The forces which govern the incidence of conflict and the scale of death are still localized, traditional ones: genuine if senseless conflicts, deaths occurring on a scale with at least some reference to the objects of struggle. But in the post-Second World War period, as the world situation casts its shadow more and more on local conflicts, so the general technological environment of large-scale death is imported into them and the localized effects diminish in importance.

In China, the physical environment created by the big guns has not existed to a very large extent at all. In China, of course the natural environment was sufficiently deteriorated not to require the massive technological creation of a death environment.

Small Arms

The use of small arms is much wider than the limits of formal wars or conflicts. Big guns are used within the context of a formal war, and indeed often dominate the context and create their own environment. This is probably not true of small arms. There is always, I believe, a controlling system or factor stronger than the weapons themselves. This is clearly evident in the case of *formal executions*, where the legal or pseudo-legal process decides death for every individual; death is certified in advance. Execution can be by a number of means – strangling, guillotine, hanging – as well as by shooting. But it seems unlikely that the executions of this century would have reached such numbers without the rifle and pistol. Pulling a trigger is so easy. The uniquely twentieth-century characteristic of these killings is the scale on which they have occurred. The sinister auspices of state interrogations, trials, summary executions are not new, they are as old as human records. The scale is quite new, and it is of course the scale of military operations and of massacre.

SMALL ARMS

Formal execution, 4 m. deaths

Massacre, 6 m. deaths

Combat, 14 m. deaths

If the massacre by big gun and the massacre by formal execution are rationalized by their apparent connections with traditional human activities – 'fighting' and 'war', 'punishment' and the 'legal process' – at least in the massacre by massacre there are no such hypocrisies to obscure the simple truth. Administrative or military orders, men with guns, selected victims, killing: that's the simple recipe. In listing five major areas of massacre with small arms, I shall indicate associated areas where massacres on a smaller scale have occurred, and the approximate figures relate to all the areas mentioned.

The last and largest category of small-arms deaths is those that occurred in military *combat*. My impression is that, on the basis of about fourteen million deaths, half of these would be in the two world wars, and the other half in other wars including those in China. Of the small-arms deaths in the First World War it is likely the preponderance were in situations where the massed firepower of small arms was used as a means of massacre auxiliary to that of the big guns. This would also be true of Russian combat deaths in the Second World War, and somewhat less true of deaths on other fronts. In the spectrum of smaller wars over the century the pattern would be more erratic. It is probably safe to say that at least half of all the deaths from small arms in the major and minor wars had the characteristics of massacre in environments dominated by big guns.

Recipe for massacre

Administrative or military orders	Men with guns	Selected victims	Number killed
Suppression of minority and other *ad hoc* orders	Turkish Army and others in 'small' wars	Armenians and others	1m.
Enforced collectivization and other administrative tasks	Russian S.P.	Peasants, camp prisoners, etc.	1m.
Reprisal orders and other law-and-order measures	German Army	People, random selected	2m.
Orders to suppress and destroy Jewry and other groups	German S.P.	Jews, Gypsies, old and sick people	1m.
Three-all Policy and other *ad hoc* orders	Japanese army and other armies in the Second World War	Peasants and others	1m.

Approximate total 6m.

It becomes necessary to make a distinction between formal combat and what we understand by conflict. Presumably, in conflict in the individual sense, there is some kind of equation such as equal opportunity for both parties or at least a feeling of such, or that the outcome should be dependent on some kind of skill. Conflict in this sense does not exist where people die from privation, or from the big guns, or from the various massacres of small arms. Only in about half the deaths from small arms in combat situations is there the remotest possibility of a conflict situation having existed. If we add to this the category of demographic violence where there is clearly a large element of conflict, we have a figure of about ten million deaths where a situation of conflict *might* have existed; that is to say, in less than ten per cent of all the man-made deaths of the century.

Demographic Violence

Each of the three cases I have noted, the Russian Bread War, the Chinese anti-bourgeois campaigns and the Indian Partition riots – accumulating to a minimum of three million deaths – might be looked upon as escalated forms of micro-violence. That is to say, to some extent they have the character of ordinary civil violence. Yet in each case there is a macro-element in the organizational structure of the event as well as in its incidence, in the form of an instruction or recommendation from the centre. In each case an official pronouncement, coming at a time of transition between two systems of government, leads to a violence which reflects the clash between the two forms of government. This reminds us that even in an age of macro-violence the violence of 'the people' remains micro-violent, that is taking the form of frequent individual and occasional mob violence which *never* approaches the dimensions of macro-violence *except when organized by the state*. Feelings of violence in the people are only united into a mass in the fantasy of scholar and politician. Thus we have the grotesque paradox that many respectable statesmen, in their fear of 'the people' or 'the masses' or 'disorder', recommend that the best way to keep them off the streets is put them in uniform – the very action that unites vast numbers of people in the potential of macro-violence!

The very exceptional nature of demographic violence in the spectrum of macro-violence – the fact that it involves hand-to-hand fighting reflecting direct conflict, aggression, fear and struggle in the individual – leads to a necessary question. Do the technologies of macro-violence, with a few exceptions, lead to situations, and ultimately to a general situation, in which violence may explode or proliferate without reference to conflict, aggression, fear or struggle? Can macro-violence become completely divorced from human psychology and motivation? If it can, then it calls for a completely new dimension of inquiry, for most studies of violence assume a link with aggression, conflict, frustration, boredom and other human conditions.

Aerial Bombing

The number of deaths may be a good deal in excess of the one million I have calculated, but it is most unlikely to be more than two million. The peak level of deaths for an individual city is about 200,000 and the main victims were Dresden, Hiroshima and Nagasaki, chief targets of Allied terror-bombing in the Second World War. The deliberate bombing of civilians was the chief source of deaths in volume, and other cities attacked in this way during the Second World War (including the Sino-Japanese war) were: Coventry and other English cities; Rotterdam and other Dutch cities; Warsaw and other Polish cities; Stalingrad and other Russian cities; Shanghai and other Chinese cities; Frankfurt and other German cities; Tokyo and other Japanese cities.

In the bombing of cities the technologies of violence are destroying the technologies of peace. In the early days, bombing was similar to the shelling of a city, that is the city happened to crop up in the strategic plans. By the time we reach the atom bomb, Hiroshima and Nagasaki, the ease of access to target and the instant nature of macro-impact mean that both the choice of city and the identity of the victim has become completely randomized, and human technology has reached a final platform of self-destructiveness. The great cities of the dead, in numbers, remain Verdun, Leningrad and Auschwitz. But at Hiroshima and Nagasaki the 'city of the dead' is finally transformed from a metaphor into a literal reality. The city of the dead of the future is our city and the victims are – not French and German soldiers, nor Russian citizens, nor Jews – but all of us without reference to specific identity.

Chemicals and Other Advanced Technologies

About the asphyxiation of between one and two million people by poisonous fumes in specially prepared chambers and vans, there is little to be said that has not already been said. It should be studied in direct physical detail as recorded in several books and the reader will then find if he has not already done so that there is no need to compare it with anything else in order to get it 'into perspective'. Since then science and technology have proliferated the technologies of macro-violence to the extent that every new technological development has a death-application as well as a life-use. If you explore the ocean bed and contemplate its human uses you also devise a means of devastating the ocean bed. If you discover how to isolate germs and viruses for protective purposes you also proceed to concentrate them into a technology for killing a million people. If you can deaden the nerves to lessen surgical pain you can also paralyse the nerves for hostile purposes, and modify your technology to produce various degrees of agony and types of death. Whilst scientific discoveries and technologies often remain hypothetical and open-ended for a considerable time while their life-uses are being explored, the death-application has the advantage of unquestionable effectiveness. The technology can thus instantly become a closed system and acquire that aura of magic and power which has been sought through the ages by villains, charlatans, psychopaths and fools. Thus, for instance, the attempt to connect the subtle detail and variety of human behaviour with physiological processes is delicate – difficult – hypothetical – frustrating – open-ended. But if you approach it from the angle of the *death-application*, you can most certainly by drugs and surgery ensure the deadening of great areas of human behaviour, and thus become a magician freed from irritating difficulties.

Such is the romanticization of technology, like the old romanticizing of nature, that the technologies of macro-violence are actually glamourized in modern fiction, with the glossy inanity with which overfed, stupid aristocrats used to dress up as swains and shepherdesses. These corruptions are beginning to eat back at technology so that, in addition to the city of the dead as a future arena of self-destructiveness, we have the possibility of human technology destroying itself at source.

10

THE DEATH PROCESS

THE DYING BODY

THE skeleton structure of the death machine provided by the technologies of macro-violence conditions environments to produce death. The individual *death process* may then be deduced to some extent from the overall process occurring in specific environments, and a look at these may help us to put the flesh of dying on the bones of death.

Privation could be described as a one-dimensional version of some basic human experiences: work followed by recreation and sleep; cold followed by the warmth and comfort of indoors; hunger followed by a leisurely filling of the belly; illness followed by recuperation, care and health. Civilization guarantees the complete experience to such an extent that the hardship is actually enjoyed in delicious anticipation of the restorative. In a privation environment sleep, warmth, food and care are doled out, if at all, in such quantity as to maintain the functioning of the body without restoring its substance. The body has to continue to function while wasting away. The structures of civilized society work to minimize any privations that occur, to limit them to one type, shorten the timespan. For the individual who strays from the private and public centres of succour and restoration, attempts at least are made to rescue him. In the little society of the privation environment, no such centres exist, indeed the very core and ethos of the system is the application to the body of the multiple pressures of deprivation over a sustained period. The objective factors of the *deathspan* are the duration of the privation system and the range of pressures existing within it. Up to two years for siege, economic blockade, man-made famine, scorched earth, transit and combat privation; up to five years (duration of war) for ghettoes, occupation, prisoner-of-war and concentration camps; rather longer, say eight years (duration of general hardship), for war and civil dislocation; and up to twenty years for the labour camps. These are the maximum deathspans for particular systems, the slowest deaths possible. In practice, the maximum period for the great majority of people is likely to be about half the figure noted, because of the intensity of the actual pressures at work. These are seldom single pressures. For instance, the most fundamental deprivation, lack of food, even when operating most directly and simply as in economic blockade and man-made famine, brings disease with it as well. A further factor in reducing deathspan is the existence of areas of particular intensity within the system. The complex pressures of the camp system – low rations, indifferent medical care, minimal shelter – is taken to a total degree in some of the prisoner-of-war camps for Russians where there is no food, utter neglect and no kind of protection from the elements; and to a lesser degree in some of the concentration camps. The maintenance of family structure in the ghettoes sustains a certain network of care, but the improvised social services lead to recurrent epidemics and so an intensity of disease is added to the pressures of malnutrition and forced labour. A third objective factor, which in a vast number of cases reduces the deathspan to a few months, is the initial impact of the privation system on bodies accustomed to civilized living. In the cases of siege and scorched earth, there is an obvious time-lag between the initial impact of the privation pressures and the improvising of survival structures by the social body as well as the building up of resistances in the individual body. In the time-lag, death for many. In the case of the war dislocation in China, the privation works its impact on structures which are already precarious and have very little in reserve, and the time-lag becomes chronic. Even more chronic is the failure of structures in the Russian Civil War period where the impact of privation, instead of stimulating resistance, merely crumbled the old structures further and baffled the new structures which should have been organizing survival. The pressures of privation are summed up in the Russian labour camps. A standard range of pressures – forced labour, minimal rations, indifferent care – is applied with complex variations in different camps, to the extreme where survival rations are obtained only in return for high work-norms, and neither rations nor medical care are available to those who can no longer work. In this environment – random death – many do not make a long-term adaptation to the impact of privation, and die within six months or a year. But in the camps of the Arctic and Siberian wastelands the whole system is on a different level – total death – because the natural environment itself is so arid and frozen as to be hostile to human life. To work in the open without special protective measures is a form of constant exposure to death.

How long is a slow death? Most privation deaths may occur after periods in the death environment ranging between a few months and two to three years, with the numbers perhaps fairly evenly spread along that range because of the different objective factors working in the environment. The deathspan is also a subjective matter since it is not usually clear why some people last longer than others. If we think of the *before, during* and *after* aspects of the death process which I mentioned in the introductory chapter, the deathspan is partly the *before-death* period of suffering the pressures of the death environment, and partly the *during-death* period, and the relationship between the two varies. It is clear that the pressures of some of the death environments have reduced some bodies to a condition of minimal functioning in which there is virtually none of that surplus of feeling and thought from which we get our idea of the mind and spirit. These are sometimes called the living dead but I shall call them dying people. For them the critical period of dying lasts a very long time, so long as to be meaningless, and the moment of death perhaps makes little difference to them (although some such people have been nourished back to body and spirit by rescuers: dying people are not dead). Other people have a very different experience. A period of months or years in the privation environment culminates in the impact of a particular situation – disease, illness, total withdrawal of food – which brings about the critical period of dying in abrupt and acute form leading to a highly conscious moment of death. This may be accompanied by an actual change of environment such as in transit or combat privation deaths.

Some of those who went to the gas chambers were sent there from a survival environment, so that a brief period in the death camp was their total experience of the death environment. But many had already spent months and years in the attrition of the ghettoes before the critical period of dying in the gas chambers.

Similarly, in the hardware environments of the big guns and small arms, there are often severe pressures on the body before the blow or impact causing death. Also, the larger the scene of death the more likely it is that men will die neglected from wounds, thus prolonging the critical period of dying. I say 'men' advisedly, for this applies only to the military battlefield. In the case of massacre, to which women and children are equally subject, you are supposed to die from your wounds anyway – it is your duty to do so because you are being massacred. As multiple pressures and varying deathspans are typical of the privation environment, so the more abrupt and violent deathspan of the hardware environment is characterized by multiple wounds and variations in the critical period of dying. The shell shrapnel of the First World War, jagged pieces of hot iron, was usually large enough to cut across different organs of the trunk or abdomen and produce multiple injuries at a single impact. Shell-blast, shrapnel's twin, also destroys different parts of the body at one blow. In the Second World War, shrapnel and indeed the whole range of heavy weapons, was much lighter in impact. Hence the proportion of wounded to dead was much larger. Hence the proportion of dead with multiple wounds was also, perhaps, much larger. The Second World War, saw the arrival of penicillin and the other 'wonder drugs' which help the healing of wounds. But it also saw the arrival of a disruptive and explosive capacity in the war machine which in the intensest areas of death such as the Russian front carries millions of men – yes, *millions* of wounded men – beyond the reach of medical help. There is a principle there, something like *the destructive capacity always outreaches the remedial organization*. As for medical aid to those wounded in massacre attempts, that is of course strictly forbidden by human logic.

Getting right down to the death process in the individual body, these categories bring us to: *before-death*, the body of suffering; *during-death*, the body of dying; and *after-death*, the body of death. I had meant to set out physical descriptions of these in terms of quantities, percentages, types of suffering, wounds, disease, in proper diagnostic language. Apart from difficulties in the way of doing so, it occurred to me that medical description and other objective measurement of parts of the body is only meaningful in relation to the attempt to prevent or cure disorder. The response of the body to freezing temperatures is of intense interest to us in contexts of survival such as Arctic exploration. In the context of a death camp the information would be of purely descriptive value since the victims do not survive. Therefore, whilst a pathology of the violent dead is essential to the general theme of preventing recurrence, the relative uselessness of diagnosis in specific cases raises the question, how much quantifying and structuring can the subject take without being completely distorted? There is no doubt that the procedures of measuring and quantifying can become compulsive, to the point of what I would call *metromania*, where the measurement is taken for the thing itself and indeed displaces it.

The human body is universal, but that does not make it a planet of flesh. The body of suffering is universal: that does not mean it is an emaciated monster. The universal body of dying is neither a stranded whale of agony nor a zombie of living death. It is true that some people have perceived, in the remains of the death camps, in the uncovered execution pits, in the corpse-high battlefields, a monstrous body of death, but they have never managed to give it any meaning except in terms of negation and emptiness: the persuasive meaninglessness of the quantitative vision that created these horrors in the first place. The universal body of death is not expressible in terms of factitious quantities.

It would be possible to quantify and describe the suffering, dying and dead bodies without once touching on the focal point of the death process, the moment of death. What expertise might be erected over this emptiness! What pale fluttering mortqueans might jargon in on the subject, to explain to us what death (reduced by skeletal diagrams to physiological processes) is, to scientize and consumerize, to branch out as death counsellors advising tranquillizers and regular healthy visits to the cemetery – 'With the correct partner and a frank adjustment to the difficulties, Mr Frisby, there is no reason why you should not continue to be dead for a very long time.'

So much for the science of death and its experts. All men can refer equally through the universal body to the moment of death. By this vision the civilized structures, whereby hunger and cold are supported by the promise of satisfaction, become transparent and we can see the one-dimensional body of suffering, deprived of food and heat. Of the senses only sight is left, touch has disappeared somewhere along the nerves, the others are stuffed with stench, muffled in hunger or sealed in deafening noise. To what purpose should I list surgical parts and the complex names of diseases? Rather I should look through all such measurements to the one-dimensional body of dying: alone, unknowing, perceiving only the external bleeding, swelling, vomit and the miasma of pain.

If you look at the spread-out fingers of your hand and think that the world will exist without you . . . if you can grasp this reality while your hand trembles slightly and pulses with life . . . then you may experience the emotion of death, which lyric poets have expressed for thousands of years but which every man has at his fingertips. If this is a way of apprehending the moment of death, how can I comprehend the pressures of, say, forced labour through that emotion, since even the most awful work has its satisfactions at the end of the day? Counting the dead is not back-breaking work but the records are patchy and you have to think yourself through a morass of slippery doubts to the feeling that a figure is reliable. Nevertheless the body justifies its day's labour by claiming, even joyfully, the rewards of sustenance and simple relaxation. It is at such moments that an inner voice says, how can you play about with the dead in this unfeeling way . . .

your pretensions to knowledge are absurd. You are dealing with thousands, millions and yet you do not know or understand even a single one of these human beings, nor are you fit for understanding. An image seeps into my mind, sometimes it is the oval shape of a head and trunk, emaciated, dark with suffering; sometimes just a blurred feeling of bodies dying. Every structure inside me, false or good, breaks down and I weep, not for humanity but for those whose bodies have without justice suffered for the errors of their times, whose bodies have died without care or self-knowledge or the grace of age, whose bodies have been found dead by careless functionaries or random bugs.

As for the body of death, in the cases where it survives it is disposed of in something like the usual way, except for some bodies in the keeping of the Nazis. The corpse technology of the Nazis – separation of bones, hair, gold teeth and minor attempts to make bones and skin into consumer products for the domestic German market – was apparently an attempt to make death a purely quantitative matter. Strangely enough, in the spectrum of deaths from macro-violence it is quantitatively insignificant, although it has become with Hiroshima (also quantitatively not remarkable in its context) the ritual symbol of the attempt to identify death as a quantitative phenomenon.

If you have ever visited the slaughterhouse you have surely noticed that the cobbles or flagstones run with a mixture of blood and dung. Yellow gristle and other exposed tissue looks oddly unconvincing and useless. Miscellaneous bones lie about with no reference to the living wholes they once belonged to. You may have observed a certain unity in these arrangements.

THE DYING MIND

So soon as a religion, a state or a philosophy claims explicitly or implicitly to pre-empt the central spiritual reality and identity of the human being, that is the beginning of the death of the mind. How can this trick be performed? The key is the *refinement* of the idea of spiritual existence or spiritual identity into a concept which is entirely divorced from the body, so that it is something like a plastic bag filled with ether, rather like primitive ideas of the soul. The spiritual identity of the human being is simply his fundamental human identity, his desire to eat well, breathe freely and demand justice: quite inseparable from his physical being, and quite simple. If you convince a simple soul that his spiritual being is highly refined and rarified you might persuade him that it cannot be allowed to remain in his keeping – that it belongs in the plastic bag. Thus, whilst this piece of arm-waving illusion is going on, you persuade the poor fellow to let slip something far more precious, which you have not even mentioned – his simple human identity, his desire and need to question your motives in your physical dealings with him.

The traditional Christian society assigned to the poor the highest possible form of spiritual identity, but promissorily; the actual transaction was to take place in another sphere – appropriately enough the 'spiritual sphere'. So far as worldly life was concerned, the poor were simply used as material, their spiritual existence being denied in practice. Traditional Marxism also materializes its opponents, denying them any spiritual existence or motivation. The scientist achieves false objectivity by virtue of a peculiar condition: the fact that human beings always *assume* their own spiritual existence and validity, and do not need to declare it or enter it into the argument. For instance, if I am looking at human beings as mechanisms and am faced with the question, are you yourself mechanical? then I can see at once that my position is false. But who is to face me with myself? If I have sufficient power, or influence supported by custom, my words begin to become 'reality' and my logic a structure of power.

The announcement that the human spirit is finished and that all that is left is gross materialism is usually, as I perceive it, the nostalgia for a lost identity. In our day, for example, it is hardly possible to enjoy the full flower of bourgeois living, and many middle-class people bitterly regret this. Some of them even assert that what has replaced bourgeois living has no spiritual values. This tendency to materialize *the other*, to deny its spiritual existence, is a fascinating human constant.

It can also happen that the reaction or protest movement against a former establishment can itself become arrogant enough to pre-empt spiritual reality. So we get ideas like 'the death of God'. And we are always hearing about the death of poetry, the death of the theatre, the death of the printed word – all aspects of the death of the mind. It's amazing with what frequency those wishing to promote a new fashion begin by announcing the death of something or other. It is true that some things do prove themselves to have been ephemeral and disappear into the maw of time. But when we are told yet again that because of some new cultural phenomenon – photocopying, television, Rotiss-o-mat chicken-frying – a vigorous human tradition is 'dead', then a good first reaction is to ask oneself: *does* the mind die, is it something that curls up into a terrified ball at the first sight of a mechanical process, and dies?

A ready-made deathtrap for the mind is the idea of people as a mass or 'the masses'. Fear of crowds has always been a common emotion amongst the upper classes. Both of these attitudes involve a projection of the self on to an external reality – 'the people'. We might say that the latter attitude is an emotion rooted in the fantasy of an individual temperament or small élite class: that is a *qualitative* fantasy since it takes its colouring from the individual emotion. The conceptual fantasy of 'the masses' on the other hand, since it purports to take its shape from a measurement of the external object, might be called a *quantitative* fantasy. The qualitative fantasy projects the self on to the crowd in the form of fear; so that, although dangerous, its elements are at any rate identifiable. But when the quantitative fantasy projects the concept 'masses' on to people, we must ask, what happens to the self in which that concept is rooted? Now, a famous ecologist claims that he can sustain any conversation on pollution by simply repeating the phrase, Where does it go? The chemical waste is dumped by the manufacturer – Where does it go? Into the river – Where does it go? The river takes it to sea – Where does it go? and so on. The polluting material never actually disappears. So, where does the self go? The self never disappears, and if its whereabouts are not evident we are entitled to ask what it is polluting. With the quantitative fantasy of conceptual thinking, the originating individual may declare how the concept is modified by self in his own case. But the more successful the concept, the more likely it is to be adopted by the academies and become an *institutional fantasy*. Where does the self go? And the more the academics influence the powers-that-be, the more likely the concept is to be adopted by government and become an *official fantasy*. Where does the self go?

Whilst qualitative fantasy, short of sheer bigotry, often expresses a lively sense of its own limitations, quantitative fantasy, it seems, brings with it the delusion of knowledge, and in its certainty chokes off the sympathies and will not allow them to travel to the object. We do need to project our *selves* mechanically, through measurement as through the telephone, the cable, the airline. But the purpose of mechanical projection is the first stage in making the human connection, the final stage of which is hopefully the flow of sympathy and understanding – the expansion of the world! Where projection stops at the mechanical stage it is not only useless but self-frustrating – it shrinks the world!

I may illustrate the modern nature of this particular death-of-the-mind syndrome by reference to my own etymological researches. After laboriously conceiving the term *metromaniac* (used above) as a description of someone obsessed with measurement, I rushed to the dictionary to find out whether anyone had thought of it before. They had. It was coined in the eighteenth century to describe young men with a passion for writing verses. If I was disappointed with the precedent, I was delighted with the analogy. For I had clearly gone through the same process as some eighteenth-century writer in seeking a term to describe a passionate but arid intellectual activity of the young. In those days it was a binding of feeble fancies in the fetters of poesy – perhaps as good a place as any. In our day, by an unfortunate involvement, the conceptual fantasies of the young are enticed into the dead landscapes of *institutional fantasy* and even *official fantasy*. Where does the self go?

Much manipulatory pressure has gone into trying to make aspects of people's behaviour unified as a mass. But the only examples where it can even be claimed that the whole of the human behaviour and personality have become mass behaviour and mass personality is in the environments of death created by the technologies of macro-violence. We may examine the extent to which the claim can be substantiated, by looking at the pressures of these technologies on human identity.

The following sociology of the dead is my fantasy.

The first table below classifies the public dead in two ways – *social origin* and *traditional public identity or role*. If we look at the table we can see that social origin, in terms of being *urban* or *rural*, is a very simple and relaxed kind of identity. I have not polarized the whole into these terms, instead leaving a substantial section of *mixed* origin. This is partly because it is difficult to distribute them accurately in the urban and rural categories – but it is a useful inadequacy, for it emphasizes the transitional nature of the period we are dealing with. Also, it might help us to avoid a very popular pseudo-scientific fallacy – that an urban consciousness or identity inevitably follows from the formula of living in an urban environment. For example, if we distributed

	Social Origin			
	Mainly URBAN	MIXED	Mainly RURAL	TOTAL
	Millions of deaths			
Traditional Public Identity or Role				
SOLDIER		26	12	38
CITIZEN	25	10	4	39
PEASANT			27	27
JEW OR RELIGIOUS DISSIDENT	6			6
	31	36	43	110

the *Soldiers* of mixed origin no doubt a majority would go into the *Rural* category. However, it is well enough known that the bulk of the citizen armies of the century have been made up essentially of *the poor* – men for whom being a soldier was their first public role, both in the sense of social commitment and of actual experience. This would tend to be a much stronger factor in determining consciousness than the question of whether they were urban poor or rural poor.

The *Citizens* from a mainly *Urban* origin are mostly Russians, at periods when Russian cities were particularly unstable and vulnerable owing to large recent influxes of population. Indeed if we take the whole 110 million we might say that a couple of generations before the events in question two-thirds of these people would have been country-dwellers, whilst a generation after two-thirds of them would have been confirmed city-dwellers.

In other words the question of urban or rural identity was generally in a state of flux and it is the instability that is the most significant factor.

The traditional identities of Soldier, Citizen, Peasant, Jew, are much sharper definitions of public role, but because they are so traditional it was possible, in fact usual, for the individual to accept such roles with very little self-consciousness. Yet if we think of the process of natural alienation we can see that each of these roles had attached to it not simply an alienated form, but two distinct versions, equally unreal and corresponding to the dichotomy of good and bad. The *Soldier* was either a scruffy, dangerous slouch who brought trouble to your district and especially to your daughters; or he was a brave, brisk fellow who performed gallant services for society. The *Citizen* was a shallow, self-indulgent gullible trick-merchant; or he was sober, industrious, community-minded. The *Peasant* was an animal or a rustic swain. The *Jew* preyed on nice Christian society, or he sustained through suffering a mysterious and noble body of knowledge.

The convenience of such alienated images was considerable. You could choose the good or bad image depending on which side you wished to support. You could avoid looking at the condition of the peasantry by emphasizing their rustic swain-ness. You could borrow money from an upright Jew and refuse to pay it back to a parasitic Jew (same fella). At the extreme of self-indulgence you could manipulate these images in a quite conscious way according to your own needs.

Thus all of these public identities, although traditionally solid if not secure, were already highly vulnerable to manipulation in the kind of societies which existed at the beginning of the twentieth century. What we may now observe is how these identities were transformed by the pressures and logic of modern violent technologies and ideologies.

Traditional Public Identity or Role	Alienated or Processed Identity			
	Mechanthropoid	Paranthropoid	Randomized	Total
Soldier	32m.	6m.		38m.
Citizen		13m.	26m.	39m.
Peasant		10m.	17m.	27m.
Jew or religious dissident		6m.		6m.
	32m.	35m.	43m.	110m.

We can see that the Soldier has been transformed into the perfect creature of the machine, a person who both serves the machine and is destroyed by it. There is nothing metaphorical about thirty-two million mechanthropoidal deaths – one million from disease, the rest from big guns and small arms in combat. The paranthropic process is applied over a wider range of identities and technologies: to the soldier selected for death in Russian labour camps and German prisoner-of-war camps; to the citizen designated an enemy of the people and sent to Russian labour camps and Nazi concentration camps, and killed in the demographic violence and formal executions of China; to the peasant massacred, starved and deported to labour camps in the Russian collectivization; to the Jew deprived, starved, gassed and shot in Europe, and the religious dissident sent to the labour camps in Russia. The randomizing of identity – that is, death brought to you in your home because you happen to be there – requires an extension of the mind, an ingenuity in devising technologies, which has by no means run its course. For citizens, we have civil dislocation, military occupation, economic blockade, massacre and execution, demographic and transit deaths, aerial bombing. For peasants we have war dislocation, scorched earth, massacre.

I said an 'extension of the mind'; or did I mean the death of the mind? At what point in the death process does the mind begin to die, and whose mind dies first, that of the deviser and user of death technologies, or that of the victim? At what point does the individual, starting no doubt from the womb as a painful single identity, consent to become part of a 'mass' of behaviour?

I can only offer contemplation of the individual in his simplest form of identity, that of man woman or child, as pressured to death by these technologies. The table opposite gives a rough idea of how this happened.

The technologies which are worked chiefly, or almost exclusively, on males are the combat machineries of big guns and small arms, the systems of combat disease, prisoner-of-war camps and formal execution, and some massacres. Chiefly, in fact, the mechanthropic or hardware technologies. A proportion of women share in some of the paranthropic systems and this to some extent reflects the political identity of women. I have assumed that demographic violence is also selective as to men and women in about the same proportions.

When we come to those which are worked equally on men, women and children the most striking fact is the range of such technologies, fourteen out of the total twenty-one. For these I have calculated men, women and children as existing in the proportions 40–40–20 per cent except in some cases where women actually predominate and a ratio of 30–50–20 per cent is more realistic. The cases where women have taken the major brunt of the death technology are those where men up to a certain age would be off on armed service and therefore absent from the location of death. These are siege, some military occupation and economic blockade, scorched earth and aerial bombs. These, as well as civil dislocation, massacre and war dislocation, operate in a random manner on people in their normal habitats – characteristics which you would expect of technologies which operate equally on men, women and children.

	Individual Identity			
	MEN	MEN with some WOMEN, say 10%	MEN, WOMEN & CHILDREN	TOTAL
	Millions of deaths			
CAMP PRIVATION				20
Enclosed ghetto			1	1
Prisoner-of-war camp	4.5			4.5
Concentration camp		2	0.5	2.5
Labour camp		12		12
CITY PRIVATION				16
Unenclosed ghetto			1	1
Siege			1	1
Occupation			6	6
Civil dislocation			8	8
DIFFUSE PRIVATION				26.5
Transit			1.5	1.5
Combat	1			1
Economic blockade			2	2
Man-made famine			5	5
Scorched earth			5	5
War dislocation			12	12
HARDWARE				47.5
Big guns	18			18
Small arms – formal execution	4			4
Small arms – massacre	1	1	4	6
Small arms – combat	14			14
Mixed – demographic		3		3
Aerial bombs			1	1
CHEMICALS–GAS			1.5	1.5
TOTALS: MEN	42	16	19	77
WOMEN		2	21	23
CHILDREN			10	10
	42	18	50	110

But there are substantial exceptions to this rule. Men, women and children are actually assigned a selective paranthropic identity in their own habitats in the case of man-made famine, unenclosed ghettoes and some massacres; and in addition to this are also physically displaced in the case of the collectivization privations, privations in the death camps and enclosed ghettoes, and gassing in the death camps. Randomized displaced deaths occur to men, women and children as refugees from military operations and scorched earth.

Remembering that at least half the forty-two million military deaths would be boys of eighteen or nineteen, or in their early twenties, the 110 million deaths would divide roughly as follows in terms of individual identity: about half the total, grown men including grandads; the rest, women and fresh boys about equal, and then, ten million children.

Now we can connect together all this stuff about identities and technologies and see where it has got us to.

During the historical period we are dealing with the basic alienated identity is unquestionably the mechanthropoid. In a time of transition from country to town and agriculture to industry, several hundred million men (probably two or three hundred million in time of actual war) have been persuaded to become soldiers in a special way. Not only are they alienated from the enemy in the traditional sense, but they are alienated from what they themselves are doing, by the complexity of machinery and system. The attractions of this form of alienation – the solidarity, the irresponsibility, the comforts of motor action and response, the communal ethos – have become deeply rooted in the emerging culture of the ordinary man. Only recently, and only effectively I believe in the United States, have the young begun to reject the mechanthropoid identity. It is ironic that some of these youngsters are able in thought to leap over the reality they are properly rejecting and accept as 'progressive' that nineteenth-century sociology which deals in 'class consciousness', the 'urban proletariat' and so forth. In truth, between these fantasies of a hundred years ago and the present, there intervenes the reality of the twentieth century. Class alienation in its critical phase, appropriate to the natural environment, has been replaced by technological alienation, which is not the vertical alienation of one group from another but the lateral alienation of people in general from the self. And if the self, the individual, has felt impulses to resist such alienation, and if the growing cities have required a true urban consciousness to combat the technologies that blindly breed from numbers, then these impulses and requirements have been muffled by the acceptance of the mechanthropoid identity in the life-experience of the post-1914 generations.

If we look at the progression of randomized identity in modern macro-violence we can see the logic of death technologies quite dramatically at work. First, we have random victims occurring from the 'accidental' effects of civil dislocation, then from the 'diffuse' effects of war dislocation. With military occupation there is a physical presence involved, but the effects are still 'indirect'. These are all what used to be called 'indirect casualties' although the scale is vaster than ever before because the technologies at work in the background are vaster than ever before. Economic blockade and scorched earth are quite conscious and deliberate technologies with random effects, although they can be made to appear 'accidental', 'diffuse' and 'indirect' because the deaths are not caused by direct application of hardware. Already with scorched earth and military occupation there is a degree of random massacre and execution, and these, with aerial bombing, are the three types of direct random killing.

Were it not for the ultimate technological developments, that position might be seen as merely having achieved a civilian dimension equal to the military in the deaths caused by war. However, the quantitative scope of the H-bomb together with the ability to reach the victim at random in his home already achieved by aerial bombing, or in other words the comprehensiveness of this technology, totally randomizes the identity of the victim. The theoretical effects of this are threefold. First, destructive technology attains the status of destructive nature at its most random and uncontrollable, that is, plague and pestilence. Secondly, the total randomizing of the victim destroys the logic of the selective victim necessary to war strategy – as already pointed out in the section on death machines – so that combative use of the technology can only occur either by accident or as an expression of the death machine itself, that is, proceeding from its own inner logic. Thirdly, randomized identity clears the path to total death, which on a global level is hardly achievable through mechanthropic or paranthropic means, both of these being too selective and controlled for that chaotic object.

In case you haven't noticed it, this randomization also implies the phasing-out of the mechanthropic form of alienation. It is true that there are still plenty of societies in the world whose citizens are prepared to accept the mechanthropoidal identity; even though Western consciousness is moving away from such acceptance, it might still be possible to impose it upon the advanced nations; there are peace-time armies in the world more numerous than ever before. Nevertheless, it is inconceivable that in the world of the future sustained macro-violence producing the kind of level of deaths discussed in this book should be conducted by mechanthropic means – that is, by masses of machinery manned and resisted by millions of uniformed men – without the intervention of the superior technologies of the H-bomb, rockets and biological weapons directed on random population targets.

Thus there are two reasons for my assertion that the mechanthropoid identity was the basic form of alienation in a particular historical period. First, the acceptance of this identity guaranteed in the thirty or forty years after 1914, popular participation in the technologies of macro-violence. Secondly, the ebbing of that participation – because the new technology does not require it – not only allows us to see it as characterizing a particular period but also throws into dramatic relief the new situation that exists.

As the human tide ebbs, the machines of violence are seen in their static, demystified reality, and associated with them are certain clearly defined groups – the scientists who devise and develop them, the professional military who operate them, the academies which sustain research into them, the government institutions which blend all of these into a self-justifying bureaucracy. It's hard luck on the scientists – to take them as the intellectual leaders in this spectrum – that they should suddenly be revealed as manipulators of the death machines. They are only doing what everyone has been doing for the last fifty years, namely, participating wholeheartedly in vicious schemes of mutual destruction.

How are we to view these unfortunates whom the fickle tides of humanity have left high and dry?

We might for instance see the sinister scientists suddenly revealed in staring pose, rigid, tight-lipped, the cause of all our ills. It is a special trick of consciousness, to freeze discovered objects as if the jungle, becoming suddenly aware of its own behaviour, should petrify with fright. Imagine a wander through the petrified forest of the sciences and pseudo-sciences, where natural forms robbed of breathing swell from hideous lumpen roots of causation, bright colours of foliage shout with guilty purpose, the very carpet of the forest needles the feet with brittle webs and nets of trivial connection, and the flat and dreamy beasts caught in that shallow glare (as from one bulb in a lab) that awaits the discovery of chiaroscuro, the mazed squirrel and behavioured stoat, the measured animals geese goats and monkeys speak their fables from the bestiary of science ... imagine it but don't imitate it. The scientists are not those stuffed creatures they imagine us to be, they are all perfectly warm, nice and innocent chaps. What we are concerned with is the fact that they are playing about with our lives, the future of our children, our right to say, not *I live because* ... (bleat of the dying mind) but *I live! therefore* ...

11

THE DANCE OF DEATH

MEN AND SYSTEMS

IT is no part of my plan to theorize on 'why' macro-violence occurs or who is to blame for it, but I shall discuss a few of the main existing attitudes in the next two chapters. In most of these a theory of causation is implicit, as well as a moral attitude. If I seem to set these up only in order to knock them down, it's not that I think they are invalid as theories. On the contrary, they are *all* perfectly valid – that's the trouble! It is the whole structure of causation and blame, in regard to violence, that is suspect. And since I want to get at the structure I shall deal with the specific attitudes very briefly.

The first might be called the *Theory of the Rational Object* and runs something like this: *The technologies and ideologies of progress, since they must develop by operating in an experimental, exploratory fashion, create pressures on human beings, and upon one another as systems, causing certain regrettable losses in human life which are inevitable as the price of progress.* This assumes that all things are secondary to the pursuit of the rational object.

The rational objects of diplomacy in the pre-1914 world were to gain national advantage and to preserve a balance between the powers. In the nineteenth century clever statesmen rationalized war as an 'extension of diplomacy'. A limited, controlled war would be followed by a resumption of negotiations. So far as wars between major powers are concerned, this rational object was destroyed in the First World War. This war involved, not the rational moves of statesmen utilizing some of the nation's resources, including armies, but the whole social and economic life of the nation. The rationale was that of the war machine whose rational object was not the gaining of a symbolic victory but the total defeat of other nations. The rational process in state diplomacy was taken over by the rational-mechanical logic of total war. It was this logic that the Nazis internalized although – illustrating the grotesque confusion of systems which prevailed at the time – they tried to fight a diplomatic war with the Western Allies and total war with the Russians. If Germany in 1914, and Germany-Japan in the 1940s, are looked upon as the aggressors who unleashed total war upon the world, it is noteworthy that each of these parties was shocked when their opponents demanded total surrender. They hoped for a negotiated peace in terms of the old rational objects. They did not understand that in the eyes of the world they had become monsters, or, to use Camus's precisely felt term, *the plague*.

Revolutionary expectations of violence, pre-1917, were perhaps analogous to diplomatic. The rational object was that a sufficient onslaught on the state would break down its structures and make way for complete social and economic change. A certain amount of absolutism and terror were expected, but only during the brief stabilizing phase of the revolution. Totalitarianism as we know it was unknown before 1917. In fact the Russian Revolution was accompanied from the beginning by a terrible breakdown in the structures that sustain life itself, and the rational object was, again, lost in the rational-mechanical logic of the total state.

Compounding the confusion of systems underscoring macroviolence was the idea of *the world* as rational object. It's probably true to say that the world has only become a rational object in any meaningful sense – for instance, knowable in physical and social detail – in the last twenty years or so. The concept we are dealing with was prophetic in nature, based partly on physical reality, partly on fantasy. The world Revolution was to be based on the industrial proletariat – a class of which the wide world was and still is largely devoid. This is a fairly typical example of a pseudo-scientific or quantitative fantasy: a well-studied sample of physical reality – the industrial proletariat of nineteenth-century England – is tenuously projected to the world at large.

The idea of World Domination has a similar blend of the physical and the fantastical. The vision of the world is that of a vigorous young provincial who sees the bright lights for the first time. In his mixture of ambition and terror he exaggerates the ruthlessness and heartlessness of the big city and in his resolve to emulate it strips himself of all modifying principle. This is the German world-fantasy of the nineteenth-century and after. This time it is an example of pseudo-philosophical or purely qualitative fantasy: the dominating ego is projected on to the world in unmodified form. The interesting thing is that at that time the world had been partially unified in any effective physical sense only by conquest, and typically by the dominating egos of Caesars and Napoleons. Since then the unifying forces of communication have made the world a truly rational object in the physical sense.

MEN, SYSTEMS AND MORALITY

The *Theory of the Moral Object*, as an attitude to macro-violence, asserts variously that *Hitler and/or Stalin are monsters; the Nazi and/or the Soviet Secret Police are vile; the Nazi Party and/or the Communist Party are wicked; the German and/or Japanese and/or Russian and/or Chinese nations and/or a few others are immoral*. This theory assumes that there is an objective standard of morality, and that deviation from this is not only wicked but is also an explanation of the vile effects.

Although this theory is obviously wildly inadequate as an explanation of anything, it is a highly popular one and it is not difficult to see why. It is deeply satisfying to be able to put the blame on others and absolve yourself of all responsibility. If you examine the hierarchical structure of this theory, you will see that depending on your allegiances you will be able to blame a very substantial and well-accepted body of people unless you happen to be Hitler; and even then you can blame Stalin or vice-versa.

Why is it that 'morality' in our age has been made to look so silly? It is true that in the midst of the violent events under examination morality can seem to be a rather effete abstraction.

It is also true that both the heroes named above dismissed morality and conscience as 'bourgeois myths'. But, dear reader, have you no conception of how pathetic and feeble is a society which does not vigorously assert every possible shade of meaning of that term? For at the last bastion of its meaning it signifies 'the way we behave towards one another' and if we have no interest or curiosity about that then we are indeed anticipating that future in which each of us as dispersed particles of matter will be obeying those various physical laws so impeccably observed and recorded by the scientists.

Morality is at the same time the dullest and the most exciting word in the language. It is dull and mechanical when we are being preached at by someone who we feel has no conception of 'the way we live now'. But if it really gets under the skin of the way we live, and works towards a critical definition of 'the way we behave towards one another' then it is the most animate of all words. The trouble with the theory of the moral object is that it is based vaguely on a Christian morality which concerns the individual almost exclusively with private conduct and is not equipped to deal with phenomena such as the Soviet Secret Police or the Japanese Army. The ethic deriving from organized religion assumes that the public sphere is taken care of by the upper structures of the religion. Even the sphere of private conduct is heavily limited, since large areas of behaviour are forbidden to the individual. Hence the individual lacks experience in extending his moral intelligence to larger areas of activity, and when he tries to do so he often thinks in terms of petty morality, or is frustrated by inexperience. Where the individual conscience is strong, public institutions evolve methods of shunting off the would-be moral activist into little fantasy worlds called the 'private moral sphere' – for example, the way the army deals with 'conscientious objectors'.

I am haunted by newspaper paragraphs about Spain, where they seem constantly engaged by the question of the length a young girl's skirt should be in public, and whether she should wear bikinis. This is always referred to as 'public morality'.

That is the naïvest definition of public morality. The second naïvest is the idea of the 'good chap in public life'. This idea dogged British diplomacy in those declining years when British diplomacy might still have achieved something useful in the world. On the assumption that a fella would extend his private *mores* – the decent but half-baked morality of a public school and a well-fed ruling class – to the public sphere, there was no need for him to extend his moral comprehension as far as the other countries he was dealing with. Thus we were constantly being told in these years that some incompetent and uncomprehending statesman was 'an honourable man', that is, his public morality was good. But for those of us to whom 'public morality' meant a proper understanding of the quantitative realities of society, his honour was irrelevant and what we perceived was a debased version of morality, a petty morality.

In an ambience where both the moral object and the rational object are debased, the confrontation of petty morality with the rational/mechanical, or any combination of these two confronting one another, is a mere dance of death. Thus pre-1914 European diplomacy, Hitler's negotiations with Western Europe, and the Hitler-Stalin pact: the diplomatic dance of death. The principle might also be applied to the relationships between governments and peoples, and between the bourgeois and the communists.

12

THE PETRIFIED FOREST

MORALITY AND MYTH

THE *Theory of the Rational/Moral Object* asserts that *There is a necessary connection, if not identity, between the Rational Object and the Moral object, and it is in the disruption or absence of such a connection that macro-violence occurs.*

This statement is somewhat truistic in form, and the real question is, which of the many attempts to relate the rational to the moral object holds the most truth?

There is for instance the idea that morality is in practice essentially based on secular myth, that is, on *mores* or customs in which men happen to believe. Clearly much behaviour comes under this definition. But there are many situations for which no knowledge of past custom can possibly be a guide; behaviour in such areas must either be chaotic or be based on highly conscious moral choice. Now, if we are studying a past arena of behaviour we can look at it *as if* all behaviour merely reflected 'the customs of the time'. This is a convenient rationalization for scholars. But it cannot alter the fact that there does exist an area of conscious and critical moral action. In practice of course critical morality also extends to areas which do not necessarily demand it but where critical morality penetrates by virtue of its own energy.

A report on the My-lai massacres in Viet-Nam in 1969 provides a fascinating comment on this. It seems that most of the American soldiers who witnessed acts of massacre managed to condone them by some such formula as 'If it's being done it must be right.' A minority objected although they were unable to prevent further acts.

The example illustrates how much of our behaviour is imitative, and how much of our 'morality' is mere rationalizing of custom – in this case going so far as to behave *as if* massacre was the custom, although these boys were not in fact accustomed to brutality in any form. It also illustrates that there is always a minority that for one reason or another is alive to a situation in a morally critical sense. The question is, how effective can critical morality ever be?

The enlistment of millions of men in armies since 1914, without moral questioning and with disastrous consequences, is another example of the need for imitative and normalizing and rationalizing behaviour to be modified by critical morality.

But is critical morality ever effective? Is it worth even mentioning it?

It is difficult to contemplate the Hitlerian and Stalinist societies without calling on the fashionable diagnosis of neurosis in the society. It is certainly true that societies can at times exhibit the rigidity typical of mental illness, and the scientific analogy is therefore a valuable one. But the suggestion of possible cure in the medical-sounding 'neurosis' or 'psychosis' is illusory, for science cannot hospitalize society and effect a cure. Indeed, if anyone ever came close to putting society in hospital it was the pseudo-scientific Bolsheviks with their 'liquidations' and the pseudo-philosophical Nazis with their 'annihilations'. Science can only provide a retrospective diagnosis; which is too late for cure: or it can provide the data for prevention, but it cannot prevent.

If the world has become a rational, knowable object, then science is our means of knowing it in that sense. But science only provides the first, mechanical stage in knowing the world. To know it in the moral sense – to make the human connection – requires an active and conscious public morality.

MYTH AND SCIENCE

Man is an aberrant species who ultimately cannot adapt to his own creations. He can subdue nature but in doing so he creates a technical environment which is far ahead of his mental adaptation to it. It is likely that, in a sense which is permanent and fatal to the species, he is spiritually immature – perhaps because, alone with his own death in a cold and unfriendly universe, he has an irresistible itch towards self-destruction. It is probable he will destroy himself and be replaced by a more efficient species, although it is just possible he may save himself by following certain scientific prescriptions.

This is a recently-developing attitude of scientists, which I call the *Scientific Inner-Man Theory*. It is certainly the most subtle and cunningly argued of all the theories. It is very difficult, if you are a member of the condemned species, to wriggle out of it. All of which has a familiar ring, surely . . . ? I must admit I found this theory most impressive for a long time, as I still do. But my evaluation of it has changed somewhat since it dawned upon me that it is none other than the Scientific Discovery of Original Sin.

Which makes me step back a pace or two, for I have no wish to get entangled in those coils. However much I went over the old arguments, about freewill and determinism, about grace and redemption, I should still end up with the same conclusion: that Original Sin is seductive, utterly beautiful, and untrue. I will merely point out (unable to resist just a touch of the old serpent) that the apple Eve ate was from the Tree of Knowledge, for which I, as well as countless others who had their bellyful of Original Sin a long time ago, are, and have been profoundly grateful.

However the real question (standing a few paces back) is this. Why is it that the structure of this argument is so unoriginal? If science is going to offer us values, are there no original scientific values which can be of benefit to us?

There was a notion going round recently that the proper scientific approach to things was 'value-free' and that to make 'value-judgements' was unscientific. But any human approach to an external object must involve a value-judgement and there is no such thing as a value-free approach. Often the scientific approach to the object involves the expression of a purely quantitative value, and at the root of every such expression there is a quantitative fantasy, that is, an assumption or prejudgement that the quantitative approach is appropriate to the object. In many cases the quantitative approach is the correct one, although it still involves a quantitative value-judgement in individual cases. Apart from individual cases, there are certain patterns of quantitative fantasy to which scientists are prone, some of which we have already identified. One is the extrapolation of the laws of matter to living behaviour. We have seen that one of the possibilities of living behaviour, in regard to conflict, is an economy of behaviour as expressed in ritual and symbol. It may be that ritual and symbol are essential qualities of life, part of its law and meaning. You will certainly never find out the truth of that if you approach it with the quantitative prejudgements of the scientist. In fact ritual described by scientists nearly always sounds like a disorder, a neurosis. The impact of matter on matter is violent, blind and repetitive. Does this mean that my sensitivity of touch, my eyes, my ability to learn and choose not to repeat – are some kind of disorder? Or, worse, that they are sentimental and trivial and not serious? Another example of quantitative fantasy already mentioned is the extrapolation of material evidence to the unlikeliest places. Scientists are as obsessed with material evidence as courts of law, and they are often no more scrupulous in its use than are special-pleading lawyers. There is a quantitative compulsion to prove a hypothesis over and over again with evidence to the extent that the evidence often displaces the original hypothesis and 'the truth' becomes a meaningless recital of physical facts. *The persuasive meaninglessness of the quantitative vision.* Those scientists who study living behaviour like to have living physical evidence, hence the cornered rat. Can you smell the fantasy of the rat? The poor little bugger is forced into all kinds of predetermined situations in order to provide the evidence for a predetermined hypothesis, just like those men who live by providing the evidence in divorce cases. I have talked to psychologists who deplore the rat, but none has ever told me in simple terms just what is the connection between the rat and us.

It's not a matter of accumulating evidence in order to accuse scientists of having fantasies. There is no reason why they shouldn't. But scientific expression, unlike other branches of culture, is almost devoid of reference to fantasy and of self-recognition in general. It's the hidden fantasy that is disastrous. Associated with this in the scientist's approach is the concealed assumption of totality – of the total validity of findings and of a general absolutism unmodified by self-knowledge. The scientist would say he does not intend to be arrogant and is only trying to get on with his work, but it is what he is not aware of that causes the trouble, as becomes only too obvious when scientific findings have to fit in with other areas of expression. For instance, social scientists produce many valuable hypotheses on the questions of conflict and aggression based on animal studies. But when the findings are extrapolated to human history, the scientist seems to become obsessed with the certainty and physicality of his experimental findings, and instead of juxtaposing them with history and arriving at some kind of disciplined and modified statement, he tends to *pre-empt* history and use it as evidence to support his findings. Which is absurd and naïve, because there is so much 'evidence' about in such an area as 'history' that you can prove almost anything by a selective choice. The same kind of distortions occur in the use of single words. For example, the word 'aggression' in the context of experimental rats might have a very simple meaning indeed. The stimulus producing aggression is simple, the form of aggression equally so. But in human societies aggression has been modified by thousands of years of complex social experience and the word itself carries that complexity. In some verbal contexts we would understand it to be close to violence, in others not remotely connected with violence. When a word arrives smelling of the laboratory or of rats it is an attenuated version of something that was once living, a skeleton at the feast of language. The ambiguities of human experience, which language tries to convey with brevity and wit, are absent from the language of science, where every paradox is a bombshell – hence the sensationalism of much popular scientific writing. For instance, social scientists often *assume* a direct relationship, even a causal chain, between aggression–violence–killing–war–large-scale death. But it is just as likely, if we are being causal, that the large wars of the century were 'because of' passivity, not aggression in individual human beings. And macro-violence has now reached technological and logical distortions whereby it could be used extensively without any aggressive motivations whatsoever.

One of the twentieth-century discoveries of science, perhaps the most far-reaching, is the scientific discovery of death. An absolute so far as human beings are concerned, in so far as it is unquestionably the end of every life, it may be viewed as the supreme absolute value. Since the atom bomb and its successors in death technology, the new possibility of total death for the species has become a reality. So that science has not only discovered the Absolute, but given it a new dimension. Now the philosophical significance of total death is that it is a permanent possibility. No matter how much death technology exists or is dismantled at any particular time, the possibility of total death can never henceforth be eradicated from human knowledge. And this is something that science can do absolutely nothing about. Having discovered and invented total death, science cannot eradicate it. And although the arrangements we have to make in order to live with total death are somewhat complex, and always will be, there is nothing of special value that science can contribute towards these arrangements. In fact the response of science to this philosophical fact is twofold. On the one hand scientists continue to proliferate the technologies of death. With quantitative compulsion they repeat the proof and create the evidence of total death, over and over and over again, building up with their bombs and deadly germs and poisons and chemicals and explosions and fissions and fusions and displacements and guns the physical basis of a whole world of death in a hundred different death environments. On the other hand liberal-minded scientists keep telling us, with the same dreary compulsion, that it is happening. But we know. Given the philosophical fact of total death, the rest follows. I do not need to visit the arms factories, the germ-warfare establishments. I do not need a helicopter tour of the Ukraine, being shown that the wind will carry a certain lethal solution *that* way, the way the heads of wheat are pointing, seeping it through the cracks in every farmhouse door. I don't need to be physically in New York to know that some streets will have a 0 per cent survival rate from nuclear fallout of a certain density. I can map it all out in the world of my head, from the skeleton structures of the death technologies used in the past, and the environments they created. The only differences are the quantitative ones of means and distribution and numbers, but the body of suffering and the body of dying and the body of death are the same. I can let the consequences of total death work themselves out in my head, for however much the outside world is seized up in its own quantitative complexities the world inside my head is still free.

But *is* the world inside my head to be free, or does science wish to pre-empt it through the Scientific Inner-Man Theory as religion pre-empted the soul through the doctrine of Original Sin? The answers to this are as varied as those of seventeenth-century or post-Reformation theology, and maybe we are facing a similar situation. As organized religion created a sphere of perfection and innocence and then made men guilty by making them feel they had departed from it, so science, having created a perfect machine of the world, accuses men of the sin of being unable to adapt to it. I don't know how the vision of the 'cold and unfriendly universe' strikes other people, but it seems to me to be precisely the Calvinist vision of damnation and the yawning pit. Finally, there is the vision of destruction, and the uncertainty among scientific publicists whether science might or might not offer salvation, and if so how, which is analogous to seventeenth-century uncertainty about whether the soul was damned, and what sort of redemption the church might or might not be able to offer.

I have no wish to discuss science as a religion, it is manifestly not, but the analogy suggests a few points. First, the arguments in the Inner-Man Theory are not scientific but ancient and mythical; but in each case they have been given a quantitative value; which raises the question, are all original scientific values of necessity quantitative values? Secondly, whilst each point in the argument is in itself a perfectly legitimate hypothesis or warning, the *totality* of the vision suggests a tension and concern about the future of science more than about the future of humanity. In this I think there is an organizational analogy with the seventeenth-century church. The Reformation having brought doubts and dissensions about certain *particulars* of dogma, the church was in theory open to a *general* attack on religion and the whole structure of values which it represented. The reformed churches feared this as much as the old churches, and it is arguable that it was in order to protect themselves from such fears that they sought out and persecuted individuals who they claimed challenged the church in this way, namely the witches. It may be that science, with the call of reform ringing in its ears, fears such a general attack, one that asserts that science and technology are not only worthless but have cataclysmically failed our expectations. I haven't noticed that science has persecuted anyone so far, but certain Western sociologists who wish to attack the technological society seem to draw back from a direct attack on scientism, which would presumably involve them in examining the dreadful scientism of sociology and possibly of Communist countries, and instead concentrate their fire on worn-out old dogmatic sins like bourgeois values, capitalism and the profit motive; an example surely of a science fearful of the ultimate criticism diverting its terror into sectarian attacks.

The cataclysmic nature of the crisis in science is demonstrated by the gulf that exists between those who believe that anthropological doom is inevitable, or that at any rate the solutions do not lie with science; and those who believe that scientific prescriptions can still be effective. This division exists on matters such as environmental pollution and overpopulation.

On the question of violence, there is a behavioural idea that crops up from time to time in one form or another, that the state should have the power to drug its citizens into submission. The latest form of this I have seen is a proposal being examined by the U.S. government to psychoanalyse children at the age of six so that potential criminal material can be taken out and subjected to long-term mental correction. This pattern of thought is rhapsodically pure, if science is purely quantitative in nature. It means that science having created a technology of violence, then decides that the cause of violence is a quantitatively determinable element in the individual human being, and that the continuous violent suppression of this will prevent violence. This religion of quantities is useful as a permanent demonstration of how far the quantitative fantasy can float a man's mind away from realities. It illustrates the three great suppressed values of quantitative science: fantasy, totality and imitativeness. And if anyone ever wishes to construct a pathology of quantitative psychosis this might be a good place to start.

But does science have values other than the quantitative? It may seem a difficult question, or even an unreal one for scientists who wish to believe there is no cohesive thing called 'science'. But the fact is that for us on the receiving end science creates problems which it cannot solve (total death is one) and is cohesive enough in practice to express recognizable values. It may be that the progressive suppression of subjective or qualitative values in scientific thought has led to non-recognition and hence the emergence of these values in a blind and untrammelled form. Let me be more specific: (a) suppression of subjective motivation has led to scientific thought being irradiated with quantitative *fantasy*; (b) suppression of the need and practice of modifying findings in the light of existing knowledge and historic culture has led to the implication of *totality* in the significance of findings; (c) suppression of the sympathetic association of ideas, an ancient and modern and very natural mode of thought, has led to a compulsive *imitativeness* in the scientific thought process: for instance, in the sense that the remedy for violence is a violent one, and in the general sense of the scientific implications that what *is* should be, that we should imitate immediate reality instead of our own desires – sometimes a good prescription but often a psychopathic one.

In some extreme cases these qualities will be suitable to particular temperaments or the motivations of particular groups, and will therefore be imposed on science in an individual, eccentric sense. But in general they are more likely to arise from the blind processes of scientific thought and to be due to a lack of light, self-reference and self-knowledge in the scientific culture. Whether this analysis is true or not, we have to use such means to look at science and technology in order to adjust ourselves to the fact that science and technology are associated with a number of disasters which are possibly imminent in the human situation and which science and technology can by no means control. The resources we need to solve *our* problems are beyond science, and science and technology have probably passed their peak in offering original solutions to long-standing and fundamental human problems.

13

THE INHERITANCE

PUBLIC DEATH

IN so far as I am able to summarize the concept of public death that we inherit, I must first emphasize that this book has been about one kind of public death only, namely that which arises from *macro-violence in the man-made environment*. I have implied that this is the 'most important' kind of violence, and so it is in our immediate present.

In the longer term, the idea of public death itself is a more important inheritance, as a concept guiding civilization, than the consciousness of any particular kind of violence. In the past, the micro-violence of nature was by far the greatest quantitative source of public death. The 'man-made environment' we boast of possessing implies a society which has brought that kind of micro-violence under control. So that we might almost see natural micro-violence and man-made macro-violence as being mutually exclusive alternatives as the major type of violence obtaining in any particular society. According to this view, as the man-made environment takes over all world societies, natural micro-violence will disappear as a threat and the long-term problem will remain that of reducing the establishments of macro-violence. This view began to emerge about the middle of our century, as more and more societies put themselves on a progressive footing and as we digested the implications of the technologies of macro-violence used or unveiled in the two world wars. It is already a few years out of date, but we can isolate this view as a stage in our evolving consciousness of the nature of violence. As we enter the last decades of the twentieth century our conception of the man-made environment is becoming rapidly more sophisticated. It is not merely a degree of human control over nature to which all societies aspire. It also involves the actuality and the threat of *over*-control, *over*-use and *over*-disturbance of nature, as well as the *under*-control of certain basic human practices. These tendencies are of course the sources of stripping the environment, polluting it and populating it too thickly, all of which are capable of leading to some form of ecological macro-violence. And that could mean a destruction of the degree of control implied in the phrase 'man-made environment' and hence a return to what I have called natural micro-violence. Indeed the future holds the threat of major macro-violence and major micro-violence about equally.

If the concept of public death is a necessary one, then the most vital analysis of it rests, I believe, on the distinction and relationship between micro-violence and macro-violence.

The significant micro-violence of the natural environment was the deep and persistent incidence of untimely death through disease, malnutrition and lack of infant care. Macro-violence, whether natural or man-made, was with a few outstanding historical exceptions an occasional shallow bump on the graph of micro-violence. Human societies traditionally adapted to these conditions. There was always qualitative protest against 'poverty' and 'injustice' but these had little real quantitative effect. The quantification of micro-violence and the formation of macro-concepts totalizing its significance and analysing its roots were conscious abstractions made by social and scientific thinkers and pressed home on society by reformers and revolutionaries. Although proceeding from a desperate consciousness of misery co-existing with affluence, these analyses were based on the familiar dichotomies of Rich and Poor, Oppressor and Oppressed, Right and Left, Exploiter and Exploited and their current incarnations of Employer and Employee or Capitalist and Worker. They were not based on a dichotomy of Life and Death because micro-violence never presented a persistent vision of total death.

The first great difference in our day is that society *cannot* adapt to the incidence of macro-violence as it did to micro-violence, because the logical end of modern macro-violence is total death. Secondly, the impact of macro-violence is quite different in character from that of micro-violence. The quantification of macro-violence is not an abstraction made by thinkers, it is a violent event having a direct disruptive effect on society. The quantities already achieved by macro-violence have been sufficient in some cases to break down the structures of society. If we extend the technologies of macro-violence and the death environments created by them into notional structures suggested by the wider variety of death technologies now in existence, we can demonstrate levels of destruction leading in direct line to total death. Thus the significance of scale lies not in a purely quantitative comparison with past violence but in its connection with the scientific hypotheses which show us the way to total death. The third set of changed circumstances is that the establishments of macro-violence are in continuous existence even when not in use.

But the most fascinating aspect of all this is the impending relationship between macro- and micro-violence. Consider the world population problem. Since natural micro-violence no longer keeps the population in balance, we have to take over this function ourselves through controlled breeding habits. Scientists having to predict danger-levels of population increase, form macro-concepts just as they once did out of the levels of micro-violence. But population is in many ways a more insidious problem than were the old slums of disease. On the one hand, since increasing population is not so self-evidently undesirable as poverty and disease it is more difficult to make a macro-impact on society with an abstracted summation of the facts. On the other hand, whilst the old micro-violence was a factor in *preserving* the ecological balance, uncontrolled population increase threatens the balance to the extent of ecological disaster, and enters our series of hypothetical levels of destruction leading to total death. On the immediate scene, the population problem applies to different countries in different ways. In some advanced nations, the economic rationale is such that the small family is the obvious option for most people. Possibly in such cases the population question will continue to adjust itself at the micro-level, that is, the level of individual decision, and will not become a macro-phenomenon. This is not necessarily true of advanced nations: I am simply demonstrating the most desirable hypothesis. In some underdeveloped nations where there is no such economic rationale, population increase has a range of possible effects. First, it can absorb production increases and sustain a level of micro-violence, or attain new levels, which defeats the aim of the developing nation to create a man-made environment. Secondly, the deflating pressures of population increase might clash with rising aspirations in the society to produce war, unstable revolution, state repression or other forms of macro-violence. Thirdly a rising population reaching the limits of tolerance in food and other resources might for a few years become itself a macro-violent phenomenon which would break down the life-sustaining structures of society and create chronic levels of micro-violence for some years ahead.

It seems that unless, in some cases, the scientists formulate macro-concepts out of the increasing population and manage to persuade people to modify their behaviour in the light of these concepts, the problem will become a macro-phenomenon and lead to a mixture of macro- and micro-violence. The same pattern holds good for the problems raised by the practices of modern industry in polluting and denuding the environment. The macro-significance of a pattern of micro-events has to be brought home in order that the problem may be dealt with at the micro-level of individual adjustment, otherwise it is likely to bring about similar types of violence. These problems apply in particular to the advanced nations, so that over-populating, polluting and stripping the environment hold threats for the world as a whole.

The ultimate conclusion reached by analysing public death into macro-violence and micro-violence is that these environmental problems, as well as our military technology – all features of the man-made environment or the attempt to achieve it – are capable of producing macro-events sufficiently violent to break down the structures of the man-made environment on a long-term basis, with the inevitable result of a chronic degree of natural micro-violence.

Since this natural micro-violence would be the result of man-made macro-violence, the distinction between 'natural' and 'man-made' violence would disappear. In fact, since the problem of reduction is the problem of controlling all these types of violence the distinction between man and nature as sources of violence tends to disappear anyway, at least as a major distinction.

There is a tremendously exciting reality to be perceived in this perspective of the future. I don't pretend to be able to see it very clearly, nor to be able to validate it very satisfactorily, but I shall express it as best I can. We seem to be moving towards a condition in which, despite the sentimental writhings about 'nature' over the last two hundred years, we shall actually achieve a *more intimate* relationship with nature than human beings have known since pre-historical times. The difference is that this will be an intimacy based on consciousness, not blindness. All human societies have passed the point of no return in their aim of achieving a 'man-made' environment. For the human individual this implies the ultimate recognition of himself as *a conscious being* who is *part of nature*, and that consciousness is natural, not an enemy or a sin. Whether this recognition is successfully achieved or not, whether we go the way of life or the way of death, it seems that an outcome one way or the other is imminent in the next phase of human development.

Although we are still only groping towards a concrete expression of this vision – and the more attempts to express it the better! – a number of implications for the present are discernible. First, we might recognize with some relief that the uneasy dichotomy of the natural and the man-made has a finite existence as a major human obsession. Secondly, that the concept of the man-made environment, as distinct from total environment, is a very temporary idea indeed on the scale of human development. Thirdly, that the new consciousness rests on the human responsibility for life and death and that this dichotomy may be the chief basis of all human values in the future.

The wider vision confirms a point already inherent in the idea of total death, namely that the only object which can properly rationalize the study of violence is death. That is to say, all other objects of thought, such as political allegiance, military or economic rationale, philosophical, religious or psychological systems of analysis have a tendency to corrupt the evaluation of violence whose significance for human beings can only be seen objectively in the light of death. Although there has been a strong drive towards this view in our societies of late it has been somewhat frustrated and diverted into sentimental, pseudo-religious and even hypocritical attitudes. This is, as I believe, because the idea of death has remained unstructured, so that a vague sympathy towards individual victims has been structured by extraneous ideologies, anti-militarism, paranoia, religious and other attitudes, which get close to but miss the point.

So soon as we incarnate death in the form of the dead, and then name and number the dead, and then structure the idea of public death into its various categories, we are beginning to see the prospect that violence holds for the human future in the light of that curiously realistic and finite version of the Absolute, total death.

EVOLUTION OF THE DEATH MACHINE

In order to outline the idea of public death above it has been necessary to mention all kinds of violence, but for the present summary we shall consider only that death machine which has evolved from the form of violence most characteristic of the man-made environment, namely man-made macro-violence.

At the beginning of these Analyses the question was asked how far the death machine might be reduced to a knowable mechanism in the factual sense, and how far it must be seen as a philosophical object, a paradigm of the outside world, the individual's relationship to which is a form of critical self-definition.

The basic mechanism proceeds in the first instance from the nature machine – a way of expressing our relationship with nature in the pre-industrial environment and in particular of referring to the system of alienation appropriate to that environment, namely natural and religious alienation. The death-breeding process links the natural to the man-made environment by mixing technologies appropriate to both, and typically by evolving from the war machine through the total-war and total-state machines to a condition chronic in the man-made environment whereby the technologies themselves take over and dictate the shape of things, create their own system of alienation which is technological and ideological, and by progressive refinement of their inner logic arrive at a rational possibility of total death embodied in scientific machines and systems.

The specific technologies of macro-violence create death environments which may be graded as survival, random-death and total-death environments. The conditions of these environments may be used to categorize and define the types of death suffered by individuals, both in terms of numbers and as connecting with the universal body of suffering, dying and death. The death process of the individual also illustrates the progression from natural and religious alienation, as in the pejorative identities of peasant and Jew, to the mechanthropoid and paranthropoid identities created by the technological and ideological alienation of the man-made environment.

So far we have described a mechanism knowable in the factual sense, that is a conceptual structure capable of expansion to contain an ever-increasing accretion of facts, and in particular to describe process and allow perception of effects.

When it comes to theories of motive and causation, we are in a different dimension. We have seen some examples to demonstrate that such theories, far from being detached explanations of the death machine, are more likely to be contributory parts of the mechanism. Those theories based on the moral and rational objects – the old bourgeois Christian morality of the natural environment and the quasi-scientific rationality of the man-made environment – are each based on a half-world of perception and represent two halves of the truth dissociated from one another. The one is quite unaware of the quantitative realities of our modern world and offers a moral vision that is petty and shrunken. The other is aware of the quantitative realities but responds to them in a purely quantitative way – the imitative consciousness at work! – which leads to a similarly shrunken vision of reason which might be called the rational-mechanical.

This suggests that the development of our consciousness not

only lags behind the evolution of the death machine, but is actually conditioned by it. How else can we explain a peculiar fact associated with the theory of the rational/moral object? This points to the split between these two and asserts the need for an identity between them. It suggests that since the world is now becoming truly known as a rational object, such identity might be achieved by a new relationship between science and morality. It is an attitude that leads naturally to the idea of world institutions and even world government. Here at last, one might think, is a rationalization that is not itself part of the death machine, but truly detached from it. Yet the common idea of world government is of a quasi-state equipped with all the weapons of destruction, and the most constant criticism of world institutions is that they do not sufficiently impose their will by force and violence. Now where do we get the assumption that an effective world culture must rest on force, and that we must measure world institutions by the marks of military success? Where else but from years of conditioning by the death machine and its operators.

I have already mentioned the evolution of the city of the dead through certain stages of self-realization – through Verdun and Auschwitz to the concrete cities of Leningrad, Dresden, Hiroshima. Is there not, following these, a spiritual City of Death in which dwell – among others – some of our outstanding writers? If *civitas dei*, the city of God, is achieved through imitation of God or Christ, presumably the City of Death is achieved through the imitation of death or of the manifestations of death. Since I have said ‘outstanding’ writers I must concede that imitation may be a necessary first stage in consciousness. But I abhor the ethos of the City of Death, that imitation is the final stage also.

Another parallel which may involve the imitative consciousness is that between certain death environments and the Lonely Universe vision which is part of the scientific inner-man theory. Our earth is fortunate in that its distance from the sun encourages life, but not all parts of the planet are friendly to men. Some of the Russian labour camps, particularly those in the Arctic circle, are situated in parts which are positively hostile, and in which men must feel almost as if they are on a planet whose conditions were not designed to receive any form of life. The plaint of the lonely universe, which some scientists are fond of, involves measuring man and other earthly life against the vastness of a hostile universe, and consequently becoming depressed about the smallness of our venture in vitality. It does recall the phrase, *the persuasive meaninglessness of the quantitative vision*; for such a vision is purely quantitative in nature. Are we not at least the self-awareness of all this blind matter? Do we not sparkle like a hard gem of consciousness amidst the universal dross and emptiness? I should have thought it was the universe that was small, cold and lonely, not us. We are warm and can decide our own size. But of course, the whole of the scientific inner-man theory is an exercise in imitative consciousness, since it is an exact replica of good old Original Sin which tells us with great gusto that *we do not really deserve to exist*.

Against the pressures of the death machine I cannot argue. How can I place mere argument against such brilliant inertia and genius for imitation? I can only assert my rejection of the epitaph (however beautifully carved):

IMITATION OF DEATH

Book Three

VALUES:
NEGATIVE AND
POSITIVE

14

NATION OF THE DEAD

WE know as much about the nation of the dead as we might have known about any living nation fifty years ago when the techniques of social measurement were still at an early stage. The population is around one hundred million. A proper census has not yet been possible but the latest estimate based on samples of the population suggests a figure of a hundred and ten million. That's about the size of it. A large modern nation. It's very much a twentieth-century nation, as cosmopolitan in its origins as the United States. The people have always been mixed, but the real growth began in 1914. Between then and the early 1920s the population reached twenty million, and steady growth over the next twenty years brought it to almost forty million by the outbreak of the Second World War. In the early 1940s the population more than doubled, with annual increases reaching peaks of 10/12 million. Since 1945 the growth-rate has declined below any previous levels since the late 1920s. This has been accompanied by a gigantic increase in the *capacity* for expansion.

Indeed, some people deny the usual bright vision that the next century will be 'the century of Brazil' – or China – or Russia, and instead assert that it will belong to the nation of the dead.

This phenomenon, like any nation and culture, is not to be summed up with a few truisms, although we shall have at any one time a vision, flawed but necessary, of the whole. We can afford to linger over different perspectives in the sure knowledge that, whatever else happens, it will not go away.

The quick packaged tour will bring out all the surface folklore of the famous regiment, the patriotic sufferings – the pageantry of uniforms and rags. Like any tourist, generous and foolish, we shall lap up the tales of the wiseacres and the old salts. Quixotic in our enthusiasms, we shall certainly enrol for that colourful up-country trip, the Quest for the Heroic Death and swell the advance bookings for the exquisite Quest for the Merciful Death. Wild horses wouldn't restrain us from a visit to the notorious Death Culture – jackboots and black suits, random bones, teeth and hair, *Arbeit macht frei,* black humour and sadism, boiled-down fat, death orchestras. The trip might even be crowned by meeting an Unforgettable Character.

– *And do you know, sitting there he told us the entire history of the country – didn't he Henry – such a charming old gentle-man –*

– *Er, dear –*

– *Such beautiful manners! and he made everything so clear. All at once I understood –*

– *Er, dear –*

– *I understood the whole thing in an instant! He explained it all in one word, what was it Henry, communism or fascism or . . . you explain it to Mr Frisby . . .*

– *Er, dear, well actually it was the World Struggle between Jewish-Communism and Catholic Democracy as Evidenced in the Historic Betrayal of the Freedom-Loving Catholic Croats by the Jewish-Communist-led Serbian Masses, but I think we ought to point out to Mr Frisby that the old gentleman had two men in white coats standing behind his chair . . .*

– *Oh Henry! and he sounded so convincing!*

A little longer perhaps . . . Stay a little longer and you have to face that difficult period of adjustment when first assumptions wobble and you grasp at the expertise of, say, a paranthropologist reconstructing some dance of death: *Backward Peasants and Progressive Killers . . . Rational Causes of Anti-Semitic Attitudes in Central Europe . . . Child Monsters of South-East Asia . . .* You sink into the dim world of the petrified forest and torture yourself with metromaniacal macrofantasies: *Man the Guilty Machine . . . Geopolitical Aspects of Urban Mass Aggression*

against Orvil Frisby, Research Student. Now you are ready for
the words of the prophet: *Lo! the nation of the dead shall come
to dominate the earth, there shall be no other nations except that
one in which the dead shall outnumber the living, and the living
shall be ghastly parodies and mockeries of what once was the flesh
and spirit of man.*

In trying to understand a nation one can make so many
desperate attempts to grasp at the whole before one acquires the
confidence to look at the facts. And that is the most delicate
operation of all, for all the facts can never be known or quickly
assimilated into one mind, they must be measured out patiently,
fed into the mind with a constant search for balance.

A survey of the landscapes might begin with that broad
diffusion of death over the plains and poor hills of China and
Mexico dislocated by war and revolution; with life draining back
from exhausted towns into the countryside and into the dissolv-
ing structures of Petrograd, Moscow, Novgorod. The peasants
of these vast provinces are a polyglot mix, in the Ukraine they
wither under the blight of man-made famine, in Kiangsi
marching armies uproot them from shallow misery and leave
them on the bare earth battered and bleached like old cardboard
boxes smelling sour in the sun and rain. You might see some
such landscapes as familiar, others with fresh surprise like
waking on a long train journey as rings of dusk creep up the hills
recalling new countries and old stories: and indeed the citizens of
these parts are cosmopolitan and have many stories. Nigerians
and Germans alike squeezed to death by economic blockade,
Armenians massacred in the gaps between large and small wars,
train-loads of Europeans dying between frontiers: Paraguayans,
Chinese, French, Americans falling to disease in the intervals of
fighting. Truly a universal nation, of which impressions must be
as fleeting as those tantalizing glimpses of quiet static things
from a train window, in the foreground rushing past and in the
distance a slowly revolving panorama. Out there are detailed
things like lanes, 11 o'clock, people crossing streets and meeting
each other behind barns. Could there be slums in that built-up
area where church spires blend with the lovely trees? Are there
people starving and being hunted through the streets like

animals? Are execution squads marching behind those lush coppices? In Shansi and Belorussia the crops burn around the massacred villages, and the Russian towns again, Orel, Kharkov, Odessa, Kiev die slowly in the multiple pressures of occupation. We rush past. When it comes to an industrial landscape you cannot see so much, apart from general greyness, black chimneys, slag heaps and waste pools, from a train window. But of course! the railway sidings, so important to those nineteenth-century places and to our twentieth-century regions of the dead. The labour camp regions, with Vorkuta and Karaganda at the very end of those railway lines that push up into the Arctic and the east, down into Siberia and the south. The thick-clanging trucks that took the living and half-living from the ghetto regions of Poland, Russia and the Baltic States; and pumped eager uniformed lads into the battle regions of the Western front, the Ukrainian front, the Don, the Caucasus, the Italian front. The concentration camps with their own railway sidings. Admittedly there are many regions beyond the end of these particular lines. Kolyma, further toward the Arctic and the east, where the prisoners went in ships battened down under hatches like cattle. Those regions further into Siberia where peasant families were left in a bare wilderness; the bare compounds surrounded by barbed wire for Russian prisoners of war; the camps and ghettoes in Poland and Germany at the end of terrible marches; the trenches and encampments where so many footslogging soldiers ended their last weary journeys. The railways only give some of the geography of the camps and battlefields of attrition, no more than they do for those industrial landscapes. To sort these out you have to stand close up to the massive blind buildings sweating steam, the trim factories unaccountably clean and neat. You look at vast chunks of steel and machinery lying in yards and ask whether the rust covering them is a sign of disuse, or whether they are so massive that they can survive the elements like scarred oaks. You wonder about incomprehensible processes and products, about strange effluences with their dirty-coloured smells, about soundless flashings of furnaces in the sky as if longer exposures of light would be audible. Who will answer such naïve questions? Not the well-dressed gentleman in the office, eager to talk but quite unable to tell you anything you would ever want to know. Not the camp guard, who will complain about the rabble of prisoners but never explain why they are there, or what is the difference between a camp region like Komi and one of the half-dozen or so major camp complexes it contains, like Vorkuta with its fifty or more camps each with a few thousand prisoners. What can it mean, this orderly technology of death? Why the product? Ask the artillery officer, so neat and confidence-inspiring with his map-case and field-glasses, how many deaths his guns can produce with one shell, with a series of twelve in a column of scattering troops over three minutes, what is the degree of fatal haemorrhage at different points on the periphery of blast? He is far too skilled at his job to know about such things! In these denser regions of the dead the very identities of the people are no longer national and tribal but conceptual, manufactured . . . prisoners, soldiers, enemies are the same in any country like workers, commuters, economic man . . . all public roles created out of the machine and the mechanthropic vision, out of the system and the paranthropic vision. Are we to accept the network of complexity such terms imply, or the even more knotty mysteries behind the knowingness of the artillery officer, the humanity of the camp guard, the clean collar of the man in the office? It would be so much easier to be back in the countryside where things are just accepted, than in this frightening in-between world, so technical and apparently self-explanatory yet so messy, so self-assured yet so utterly ignorant; half-seen from outside, half from inside, defying understanding. So wilfully resisting understanding, indeed, so eager to slobber over its own complexities, so intent on disappearing up its own anus, that it might induce in you a kind of counter-resistance, a kind of stubborn knot in the head that is only relieved by the sort of subliminal exposure to vision, to an electrifying flash of light in which you can see human bodies clawing at the air, minute insanities of consciousness stirring in execution pits, wild eyes agonizing death on battlefields, the horrible knock of the heart as a long-dying body accepts death – all in a noiseless microsecond that makes you cry out and beat your fists against a wall with fear and lean there shaken by such stirrings of madness in yourself and of the profoundest hell that lies in all men. Or perhaps not. It does not matter. You do not have to feel that particular emotion. The mind will tell you all you need to know, not from a train window for now the mind is in the cities of the dead and you can't see a city from the outside. Things happen so quickly in the city Dresden random incineration. It's all over says the surgeon burning boys, time heals over fast like an evening at the cinema, families bombed, blasted and burned, don't lay it on too thick he says in his white coat enjoying his tea somewhere else. Just one day and night of terror in Nagasaki, a spot in that ancient dark but it lingers, cripples the future. The city lays down its dead Babi Yar shoot and fall cover over shoot and fall cover over crawl shoot the act is done and burned but the layers remain. The city is knowledge. Each angled street corner is an abstraction or an algebra. Every traffic crossing shop location, service point is a draft, a calculation, a geometry. The city is not uneasy with concepts and questions, it demands and devours them unsurprised. Stalingrad is mechanthropoid, and Passchendaele, from the generating slime of explosives the stumps of houses and trees are the same inverted puzzles as the stumps of people that sprout from Hiroshima, the new inverted people of death. The city is self-knowledge, an enclosure of self-observation. In the city of the dead all the technologies of death are seen in action, in Warsaw bombs and shells, the cycle of occupation and resistance and massacre, ghetto attrition, insurrection in the sewers. Every system and concept is used until the identities of the dead are finally randomized, so that we know as we walk about enclosed in its streets and concrete and signs and traffic and movement and cafés that the city is not someone else but ourselves. Warsaw knows that its ghettoes are emptied into Treblinka and Treblinka knows its gassed bodies are the same as the fallen of the Somme. And finally no longer needing to pretend not to know what we know we realize the same consciousness of death in the three great representative metropolises of the dead, Verdun, Leningrad and Auschwitz. Indeed we may not remember a dozen cities in any country as well as we know these twelve cities from the nation of the dead.

Must this consciousness of death leave us (citadel of the mind typical of the modern city!) alone in a room where everything in the head, the angles and crossings and locations shrink to repetitive spots before the eyes, a dizziness of stopped machinery tempting us to merge swooning and mindless into concrete, grey ghosts of ourselves in the City of Death?

There is another myth, where a nation is pictured as a bursting-out-all-over place of booming cities and restless prairies, Omaha, Nebraska, Kansas, of the deep provincial peace of Milwaukee, St Louis, Columbus, golden glades of Virginia where Jefferson took giant strides of reason, drowsy space of the Mississippi, of clipper-brisk Yankee, slick-heeled Kentucky son, smart New York and flash Chicago, of the crazy glamour of Hollywood, golden California, bronze Arizona, green Maryland, of unbridled unfenced Texas, of happy banjos and swinging jazz, where the people burst out of the old strictures of living, lived, grew, exuberated, built, escaped, explored, pushed, thronged, danced . . . Whether expressed by Whitman, Jefferson or Hollywood, the American Dream is an essential life-myth of the people. We should find another name for it, less specific to America, for it is unique as secular myth, a classic model. Secular myth in this sense is distinct from sacred myth, which is a governing myth (whether manipulated by religion or the state), self-protective and unquestionable except by iconoclasm and violent overthrow. Secular myth comes from the people and in countries apart from America is known as 'folk-myth' to keep it in its place. The fictive element in secular myth is less formalized and, although manipulable, is self-critical and subject to the intrusion of fact, hence it implies a new relationship between fact and fiction.

Secular myth has two critical properties, the first being that in a society with certain freedoms and drives it is *inevitable*. It is an accretion of dreams, if you like a city of dreams which exists simply because there are people in the city. Thus it is existential in nature where sacred myth is or tends to become functional in essence. The second property is that, perhaps like sacred myth but in a different way, secular myth has *monstrous* proclivities. It grows untrammelled, it has uncontrolled appetites, it devours and consumes that which feeds it.

It will be conceded I think that the American Dream has these properties. Indeed America seems to keep at least a brace of her most valiant writers in constant harassment of the monster – harrying, keeping at bay, tactically wounding, trimming, stunning but never quite attempting the futile exercise of destruction.

Now, religious and state power structures have in the past been based on central control of the life and death of the subject, supported by a sacred myth of the power of life-and-death. The American Dream has been conspicuously successful, as a life-myth, in displacing the power of the state to control the life of the subject. But it has ignored the connection between life and death. The American Government has less control than others over the life of the subject but now finds itself with an absolute control over the death and hence indirectly over the life of its people. Only when the death-myth has been secularized, like the life-myth, shall we begin to break down the critical tensions still structuring the mystique of power.

Long, long ago the mystique of power passed from religion to the state. But for a long time thereafter it was supported by the sacred myth supplied by religion. Now science has got itself into the position of supporting the state mystique with a sacred ritual of terror based on bombs, bacteria and other technologies of death. And imitated as I believe by those writers and thinkers who retreat into a spiritual City of Death which enshrines a new sacred myth, of death without life and of life fading without renewal. The Word of that myth is the logic of Total Death.

And the nation of the dead is the death-myth of the people.

Appropriately enough, since it records in concentrated form the death of the people. Is that possible, or does it mean less than those who would shrink life back into the city of death? It means, in that survival environment of the nation of the dead, wanderer *Pavel* enclosed in a tight box of light and pegged to darkness by a bullet, it means old *Wang*'s heart leaps and flutters with shock as the floor of his hut burns toward him, and that old myth of sudden death, the *Irregular*, rots in his bed. *Peter*, the smell of cordite and slow bleeding, and *Ivan*, lungs crushed and burning in the closer environment of random death, both loving their machines. *Lydia* and *Katya*, cold and hunger, tears, breath coming and going, insides collapsing, near to total death, and as for that, *Stan* forever falling off his railway truck away from his dead children and the child *Toko* playing with his ball as the world around him begins to scream in the new light of science. They will die over and over again in thousands of minds until the meaning of death is restored.

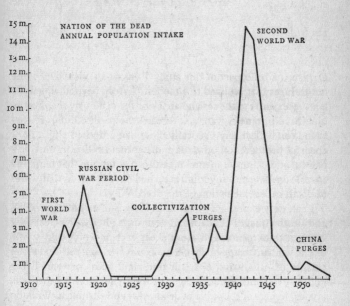

NATION OF THE DEAD
ANNUAL POPULATION INTAKE

SECOND WORLD WAR

RUSSIAN CIVIL WAR PERIOD

FIRST WORLD WAR

COLLECTIVIZATION

PURGES

CHINA PURGES

15

THE LIVING WORLD AND THE WORLD OF DEATH

DURING a brief part of this study I enjoyed a view over some hot terraces that plunged to a modest chateau beyond which the land rose gently to the sea and an island miraculously shaping the blue Mediterranean waters. To recall the precise hump of that island, on a clear day magically close like a docked ship full of cheerful presence, on other days distant and rolled in mist, is a painful and exquisite mental pleasure. Yet despite that tempting sparkle and warmth my mind returned obsessively to that world of death called the nation of the dead. Why?

I can only express my reasons as images of an emotion of life and death. Images of Mediterranean days alternating clear as if given a thick pencil and clean sheet each morning and subtle like a woman wrapped in perfume, mysterious yet attainable. Images of Auschwitz, of Leningrad rigid with cold and Lydia hollow-eyed and dying. Images of the living world, expansive, joyous, images of the world of death, stiff and shrunken. What do they mean together? At present, only an emotion but the task of describing it suddenly seems more urgent than the setting-out of the arguments I had planned for this final chapter under the headings 'Historical Perspectives', 'The False Revolution', 'Negative and Positive Values', 'A World View', 'The Shape of a World Culture'. They look impressive enough as subjects, I must admit, but what if we can describe an emotion of life and death? Perhaps we can use the tags as fuel, cast them into the flames to build and feed a steady fire. Why not?

Historical perspectives. . . . Russia has been seen from so many changing perspectives East and West that one might almost see these as cancelling one another out and leaving us with a cold but realistic view of Russia as a laboratory of the uses of violence in the twentieth century. Isn't it really quite feasible to suggest this of a country that suffered the First World War, the Revolutionary vacuum and Civil War, the 1921 Famine, the Collectivization, the Labour Camps, the Purges, the Second World War and the events of Occupation, the Deportation of nationalities, the post-war Purges . . .? The historical perspective of the living world and the world of death is as realistic a framework, and certainly a more fundamental one than a perspective dominated by views on the national character, on Marxist-Leninism, or on the mechanics of industrial change. The social life of the people would be seen, not in terms of social environments allegedly created by different political and economic systems but from the more actual level of the survival, random-death and total-death environments created by the accidents and institutions of violence.

To extend this perspective to the world as a whole calls for a Violent History, including such dimensions as the natural micro-violence that still occurs in the underdeveloped world. Other branches of history, such as Social and Economic, have already gone far beyond national boundaries but the history of violence, embedded in such ancient and irrelevant moulds as Military History, still divides nationally and is a barrier to a true vision of the real world.

The false revolution . . . As the idea of revolution comes into historical perspective it becomes clear there is a type that might be called the false revolution. This goes beyond mere reaction or counter-revolution. The classic type of the false revolution is the Nazi revolution in Germany. In all mechanical respects it is apparently a genuine revolution for it goes through all the classic motions such as liberating classes, transforming institutions, generating efficiencies; yet when evaluated against any normal human purpose or object it is seen to be negative, harmful, false. The factor which explains this paradox and which is the chief characteristic of the false revolution is that it is dominated at all stages by a principle of violence more powerful than any aim or object of the kind that usually generates and sustains revolution. In modified form, a genuine revolution might be taken over at some stage by such a dominating principle, or even by a dominating incidence of violence transforming it into a false revolution.

Negative and positive values ... In the perspective of life and death, the negative values associated with Violent History and the False Revolution are not merely causes or immediate effects. They amount to an insidious culture of negative values bound up with these phenomena in cycles of interaction and persisting powerfully in our present world. The most highly recognized symbol and sample of that culture is the Death Culture of the Nazis – the specialized addictions to death and the methodology of killing that developed in the most inbred areas of the Nazi operation. This was limited enough to be seen, had it occurred in a historical vacuum, as a monstrous aberration belonging to a particular time and place. It occurred in fact at the heart of a wider system of violence and negation visible in the range of death technologies employed by the Nazis – and these in turn are paralleled by the technologies of death employed in the Stalinist system.

The best writers of Russia and Germany have seen the Stalinist and the Nazi societies in the respective images of the prison and the madhouse. These are good images. It is not novel to observe that some of us have a tendency to imprison our fellows in our own complex of needs and beliefs, and some of us have an urge from the same sources to consign our fellows to the madhouse. And the images apply strongly to the two halves of our present world. The Communist half, distrustful and over-reacting against each other's individual impulses, has the tendency towards the prison society. The Western half, obsessed with the relativity of values and contradictions beyond meaning-lessness, has the tendency towards the madhouse society. We need these images of the prison and the madhouse, for the negative values of Nazi-ism and Stalinism are themselves not isolated in history but were preceded by the death technologies of pre-totalitarian Europe and are outlasted by the death technologies now being created in abundance by our scientists.

We cannot go on forever projecting Nazi-ism and Stalinism as the examples of violence and negative values but must bring the question home to our own present world and ask whether science is itself a culture of negative values.

There is little doubt that modern science has got itself into a position of being associated with the mechanical, with an arid rationality of intellect, and at best with the quality of objectivity as being its sole value. It is not the first time that this has happened to a culture of expression (if science is that as well as being a culture of production). It has happened to religion, literature and art many times in the past, and scientists should not be so naïve and aloof as many of them are in insisting on their 'objectivity' in the face of all criticism and behaving as if nothing is ever going to disturb the safe regular operation of that nice practical middle-class virtue. Other working virtues of the middle-class, for instance thrift and respect for the law, have been shown in the past to be capable of monstrosity if taken to exaggerated lengths. In the perspective of life and death, it is not too much to say that as science has replaced religion, objectivity has taken over from immortality as the overriding reality into which we are supposed to fit our living and our dying.

The reason these two 'realities' are so boring is that they are false, and in precisely the same way. The Christian notion of immortality is a false resolution of life and death, an assertion that they are the same. Life and death are not the same, they are different. The scientific notion of objectivity – when presented as a supreme value – is equally an assertion of identity between life and death. Life and death are inseparably bound up with one another, the one is inconceivable without the other. But they are not identical.

False identities come from acceptance of false resolutions, and perhaps a true identity for the individual lies in recognition of the true nature of life and death for himself.

The true feeling of life and death is an emotion, not a prayer or an equation. We suffer it, rise and fall of the breast, pathos, heartbeat, lyric of joy and sadness. We suffer life and death because it is an emotion, not a package of embalming fluids supplied by religion nor a set of stuffing materials to be purchased from science. To take possession of our own life and death means release from the embalmer and the taxidermist, the beginning of the demystifying and re-naturing of the intellect.

It has occurred to me whilst walking the city streets – a more usual background to these pages than Mediterranean terraces – that these crammed rows of houses are packed with more variety and concentration of nature than the long stretches of the silent countryside. We peasants who have moved into the cities in the last hundred years have made them, not towers of intellect overlooking rustic nature, but nature itself gathered into bricks and mortar and enclosed in technologies of concrete. Have we become simply a living world enclosed in a world of death? Clearly this is so for some, those who inhabit the city of death. But that city cannot be our true world of death for it celebrates death without life, just as in some shallow dreams there is no death but only life. Unreal worlds of life and death, split, not recognizing one another, false versions of the living world and the world of death created out of naïvety and fear or from an obstruction in the brain, a tumour of death.

Seeking an *answer to death* is perhaps the greatest wild-goose chase of human existence. Yet from time to time a new attitude if not solution arises out of our experience. Such an attitude is latent in the connection between *violence* and *death* which, although apparently an obvious one, has not yet been fully expressed in terms of recent experience. Violence in the twentieth century has produced the new phenomenon of *total death*. As an *idea*, total death has existed – in mental pictures of *the day of judgement, doomsday, the end of the world* – at least since the formulation of the great religions. As a *reality* attainable by human means, the science of which is a permanent unalterable part of knowledge, it originates in the notorious half-century from which we are just emerging. *Can* we emerge from the nightmare of reality and vision created in that period? We cannot create a retrospective order for the chaos of the actual events. Can we escape from the chaos of the idea that is left to us? *Total death* could mean the obliteration of particular cities or countries or regions; it could mean the collapse of world civilization or the death of the species; or it could mean the total death of the mind within a variety of physical parameters. *Total death* might be brought about by a wide range of means: by the carefully considered destruction of selected millions; by the direct and secondary effects of pollution or overcrowding; by a death-breeding mixture of every kind of human motivation acting on machineries and systems which are beyond the control of living creatures. *Total death* has a timespan overwhelming the convenient human notion of time. It can 'happen' in an instant, in a few days; it can have the monthly, yearly rhythms of traditional warfare or it could create a chronic long-term disruption of the seasons of nature and the years of human life. Its possibility is tomorrow, or in the next two hundred years, or at any 'time' in the future. *Total death* is a hard, scientific and immediate reality at the same time as being a speculative idea in search of a philosophy. No existing mental structures, of science, philosophy or religion, are adequate to contain it.

Death after all is a powerful reality. It is one of two or three fundamental ideas that condition the human attitude to existence. I think we should find, if we examined them in the cool comparative way that is now becoming possible, that some of the great religions have gravely distorted truth in order to accommodate the idea of death – to explain it away, to dodge its straightforward implications. A common result is the identification of *death* with *evil*, or with an unknowable darkness or *chaos*. Hence the rejection in the mind of death as a reality. Hence the reluctance of those who write with such vigour the history of the machines and systems of violence to mention the facts of death and to include these in their historical interpretations. Hence *our* need to *reject the assumption that reality is chaos*, to insist on *the possibility of knowing the truth about the deaths that result from our own behaviour*, to *structure our knowledge of death and deaths and total death* and bring the facts into the light of day. *Bringing into the light of day* is what happens to the soul after death, according to the *Egyptian Book of the Dead*. I made a distinction, between ancient books of the dead and the present one, of *necromancy* and *necrology*, as an indication of the different structures of knowledge of different ages. At a deeper level of truth the distinction is, I admit, a mere quibble. *Our* bringing into the light of day is different in structure but reaches the same end.

Our structure of knowledge is founded in fact. Yet the exposition of total death in terms of fact explodes the ethos of factual knowledge that is so characteristic of our age!

Total death explodes the simple *myths* of belligerent nationalism. It reduces the death-formulas of *religion* to absurdity. As an idea, it cannot be relegated to those rarefied spheres of *philosophy* where all ideas are made silly and ineffectual by the cleverness of philosophers. There is too much grim reality in it for that. As a practical reality, aspects of total death can be governed on a factual basis by a discipline such as *ecology*. But the full reality cannot, for it is too much beyond-the-predictable, its timespan is too unwieldy, to be contained within the factual parameters of a scientific discipline.

It is not surprising that the idea of total death should crash through established structures of thought. It is the intellectual legacy of a violence that crashed through the physical structures of human societies for half a century. Those who used to live by the *Tibetan Book of the Dead* would not be surprised: yet some of our most 'modern', 'scientific', 'brilliant' minds seem to imagine that we can go on living just as before, with the degradation and nothingness of the public experience expressed in terms of the historical myths and clichés that preceded it! But total death is not simply a myth-destroying reality. It disrupts more than those *intellectual* forms of mediation between man and his surroundings – religion, philosophy, scientific disciplines – already mentioned. It tears apart in the mind some of the forms of *physical* mediation that are most dearly cherished by the advanced societies. Principal among these is the arms pile.

The notion that national 'defence' rests in the accumulation of suicidal weaponry is the final surrealism of the factual ethos, for total death is itself the mocking product of this delusion.

And this great scientific proof – that there is no ultimate physical 'protection' against one's surroundings – calls in question the whole area of 'factual' mediation between man and his surroundings as expressed in technology.

Fact is not superior to myth. Technology is not more efficient than religion. However much factual and technical knowledge we acquire, we shall always have to live with the unpredictable. These are the immediate implications of total death. That is why, although this exploratory study is grounded in fact and systems, the intellectual tools I am most familiar with as a child of my age, it also indicates the possibility of *knowing* this area of reality through myth and through speculative philosophy, and future students may develop the subject in these directions, taking the factual grounding for granted.

It is easy to italicize a few phrases, more difficult to predict how they are to be absorbed into the fabric of existence. The student of total death will not expect immediate technical spin-off from his researches, for he knows the timespan of total death is not that of a generation nor of a lifetime, but of a civilization. A great deal of fuss is made about the pace at which 'modern ideas' succeed one another. But these are ideas used as technology, as closed systems of thought. The open-ended idea takes longer to absorb, it continues to breed and stimulate further thought. It was in the nineteenth century that the idea of men as gods came to us, and we still do not know what it means. The turbulence of our own century has produced advances in the idea of consciousness which we have hardly begun to absorb. And in the aftermath of that turbulence we have perforce to change our idea of death.

The discoveries of science and the rapid production of ideas-as-technology are very important and powerful and capable of bringing about the most significant historical events, such as the end of the world and endless other adjustments to life. No one can deny the impressiveness of that claim.

But with the above three ideas alone – god, consciousness, death – and the new interpretations of them afforded by recent experience, it would be possible to build a high civilization, and that is something different.

In our own period we are in the midst of a movement to recover inner values. Among these the values of death must be recycled into our vision of totality so that we may live truly in the world of life and death.

APPENDICES

APPENDIX A

NOTES TOWARDS A
NEW NECROLOGY

1. *Necrology* as a word seems to have been confined to very specific uses: an ecclesiastical roll of the dead, an obituary notice. In French, *necrologie* is used for the newspaper deaths column. Since my listing of the dead has gone beyond names, I have extended *necrology* to mean also *a structuring of death-consciousness*. Some notes on structure follow.

2. *Brief bibliography*. Most of the books I read were about war and violence but only a minority were conscious of death and of these a few seemed to share a heightened awareness from a wide range of viewpoints. These were my inspirational texts, some of them very well known.

NOVELS. *Simplicius Simplicissimus*, J. J. C. von Grimmelshausen, *The Good Soldier Schweik*, J. Hašek, *Catch-22*, Joseph Heller. Respectively about the Thirty Years War, the First World War and the Second World War, these seem to me to be in the same Central European tradition (although Heller is American) of realistic humour about war, and in a class of their own. *Babi Yar*, A. Kuznetsov. Documentary novel on execution pits and wartime Kiev. Lyrical, perhaps the best novel on straight horror. *A Day in the Life of Ivan Denisovich* and *The First Circle*, A. Solzhenitsyn. Russian labour camps, and virtually a social history of Stalinism. Masterpieces.

FIRST WORLD WAR. *Goodbye to All That*, Robert Graves. Memoir of life in the trenches. *Morale*, John Baynes. Study of soldiers in small operation. *The Price of Glory*, Alistair Horne. Campaign history of Verdun, presumably setting new standards.

SECOND WORLD WAR. *Russia at War*, Alexander Werth. Masterpiece. Two scholarly works quoted in the Statistical Appendix are I believe the chief models of what a study of a particular area of violence should be: Gerald Reitlinger's *The Final Solution* on the Jews and Robert Conquest's *The Great Terror* on Stalin's purges. If I may say so, it seems to me that all of these dozen books, including the novels, have a true objectivity, a true obsession with the object of inquiry which is often lacked by works whose 'objectivity' is really a concern with the structure of the academic discipline. It is interesting that the same kind of objectivity can be shared by works of fact and fiction.

3. During two years of writing it has seemed to me there is a growing receptive consciousness for a work on public death. For instance, some American student demonstrators used an excellent necrology in parading coffins and reading out the names of soldiers killed in Viet-Nam. But the question was, in what direction does one take structure when it goes beyond the simple listing of names?

4. The main existing structure for the consideration of death was the religious one. It was so obvious that violent death called for a new structure, a factual and statistical one, that the religious structure was seen merely as a jumping-off point. Statistics suggested more of a scientific approach, so one looked at science, and more and more critically until one ultimately reached the unexpected conclusion that *both* religion and science, being involved in what might be called the power structure of the control of life and death, were equally unsuitable as the structural basis of an objective inquiry into same. The same involvement was more obviously true of the state.

5. People ask what one is up to and, when told, they say, 'What's your theory?' Nearly everybody expected to be given a cause-and-effect explanation of large-scale violence in terms of psychological motivation. I found this widespread assumption startling. Why should it be explainable in terms of something

other than itself? When I gathered some examples of social-science research into violent behaviour I found myself carping at it so much – though the individual hypotheses were often fascinating – that I decided the material must have some common inadequacy. So far as I could determine the inadequacies were that the material was embedded in rigid structures of the academic discipline, in myths of causation, in animal behaviour; but most important, it was usually quite unmodified by any spectrum of historical fact about human violence.

6. I was therefore encouraged to think it might be a good idea if necrology should acquire its own structure as an academic discipline rationalized by the object of death, and in the case of violent death, by the objective phenomena of violence. I now believe the idea of an academic discipline to be unrealistic and even trivial but I retain the notion that necrology – structured death-consciousness – should be of itself an expanding mental structure.

7. But in what direction? In practice, in the book, I have not tried to predetermine this but instead concentrated on covering what seem to be the main methods of apprehending or knowing public death, namely through historical survey, through analysis of concepts, through myth and through statistics. It is not up to me to say which of these might be emphasized at any stage in the future. I hope they will all be thoroughly explored. I can only conclude with a few hints on possible directions.

8. Research from a statistical basis. I roughly calculated that with a budget of say £100,000 – the cost of a good piece of market research on the shape of the next car bonnet, or of a few years' exegesis of Milton's shorter poems in the universities of the West – half a dozen people of assorted disciplines and with access to other specialists might over a period of three to five years put the whole area of macro-violence on a sound statistical basis, give it historical roots and link it to the wider field of public death in the underdeveloped and ecological senses, expand the matrix of concepts and factual detail in conjunction with a continuous research activity into current and future events, and supply the social sciences in general with a wealth of enlightening and research-stimulating information.

9. The scope for individual research from a necrologica viewpoint is very great. Just to take three areas that seem obvious: (a) The violent history of certain countries – going beyond 'military history' with its clutter of *materiel* and generals and considering the interaction of all violent institutions with the developing sociology of the country – would be a fascinating study. (b) The pathology of violent death: surprisingly there is no good popular account, perhaps because the subject is essentially international. There is material in official war histories, and in particular I believe there is a rich vein locked away in Russian and Serbo-Croat military medical journals. (c) The demography of violence: surely there must come some kind of breakthrough in this subject, so that we might begin to learn the effects of violence on population – at present an area of legend and charming fairy-tales.

10. Politically speaking necrology certainly calls for world institutions, hence our political ideas are to begin with somewhat broad but here are some institutional suggestions. *Civil:* Public death institutions replacing to some extent public health bodies. *Judicial:* Life-and-death rights and identity of the individual on a world-judicial as distinct from state basis. *Legislative:* Agitation for an Obscene Technologies Act. *Judicial:* A world judiciary based on an expected death-rate for countries at different levels of advancement, with powers to intervene when the rate falls below the expected level.

APPENDIX B

STATISTICAL APPENDIX

INTRODUCTION

1. It is my impression that no statistic of deaths from man-made violence of the order of one million or more can claim a margin of error smaller than plus or minus 20 per cent.

2. This apparently rather negative finding has some interesting implications, the most important being to modify a belief some people may still hold, that official statistics in this field are precise and authoritative.

3. In my opinion by far the best statistics are those compiled by scholars who have studied the available sources and support their estimates with argument. The arguments can be confirmed or improved upon by succeeding scholars. Official figures tend to lack such civilized appendages.

4. It may be difficult for English-speaking readers to rid themselves of the notion that official figures carry authority, since the governments of Britain and the United States both claim considerable accuracy for their figures of war-dead. But apart from the First World War, when British dead approached a million, the dead-counting apparatus of these countries has simply not had to handle magnitudes of the kind dealt with in the present work. Also the types of death have been fairly simple: exclusively in war, chiefly military. The other big countries involved in macro-violence have not possessed these advantages.

5. With a minimal margin of error of 20 per cent either way, figures can be used and understood only on the basis of 'orders of magnitude'. To think of the figures as being precise and

accurate, even in the cases where it is possible to do so, would only confuse the real task of building estimates of the scale of violence chronologically, in different places and of different types.

6. Of the nine areas of man-made macro-violence which provide chapter or section headings in Book I of the text (see table on page 215) the smallest is the Jews of Europe, 5 million. The 20 per cent margin would mean one million either way in this case: about the accepted margin of error in fact. Two others, the First World War, 10 million, and the rest of the Second World War, 15 million are certainly approaching this degree of accuracy, although a refined definition of civilian deaths due to war could conceivably give estimates exceeding plus-20 per cent of these figures.

7. The estimate for other twentieth-century conflicts, 10 million, cannot be too far away from a 20 per cent margin, unless my omissions are on a vaster scale than I can conceive. Russia in the Second World War, soldiers 10 million, and civilians 10 million, cannot be too wildly out either, although the latter would again depend on the definition of civilian war-deaths. The estimates I have seen for soldiers vary from 7 million to 14 million; and I would say that the range of variation for all three of these areas *could* be about 100 per cent.

8. The remaining areas are much more problematical. It is difficult to lend much credence to those who would minimize the deaths of the Russian total state period. Unhappily, 20 million seems a conservative estimate. Wildly augmented figures have been suggested. A plus-margin of 50 per cent seems possible. The Russian Civil War period, 10 million, and China, 20 million, are also probably minimum estimates and a plus-margin of 100 per cent in both cases is quite conceivable. But that would depend entirely on the definition of civilian death in war and in the aftermath of war and upheaval, and both of these areas really invite a study of such phenomena which would expand our knowledge of the categories of untimely death and which might make our term 'man-made death' irrelevant.

9. One ends up with a statistical 'feeling' that certain estimates are reasonable, others exaggerated, and so on. My feeling is that 110 million is a reasonable conservative estimate.

Anything below 100 million would depend I think on narrowing the definition of 'man-made death' to eccentric limits. Anything above 130 million would depend on expanding it considerably, and taking into account the long-term effects of violence on populations.

10. Some readers might feel aggrieved that in our proud calculating age statistics should rest on a 'feeling'. It is painful to contemplate that despite our technologies of assurance and mathematics of certainty, such a fundamental index of reality as numbers of the dead is a nightmarish muddle. I shall try to explain how I arrived at the position of basing estimates on a 'statistical feeling'.

11. After considerable agonizing and floundering amongst the records and estimates and hearsays of deaths in the periods under study, it gradually became apparent that the hope of making a definitive contribution to the statistics of any particular period was quite illusory. That could hardly be done without detailed knowledge of the period and patient scholarship of a traditional kind. However, one emerged from this exercise with some useful perspectives, an idea of the main estimates and arguments in each case, of comparative degrees of accuracy and validity of sources.

12. Obviously, the sources relied upon would have to be secondary sources in every case, supplemented by one's own hypotheses in cases where little attempt had been made to estimate numbers of deaths. This involved the recognition that official sources in this field are not primary sources, except in those few cases where governments had an adequate system of recording violent deaths. For a similar reason, and because macro-violence by its nature tends to outstrip any existing method of calculating its effects, on-the-spot primary sources, although always of qualitative value, would not necessarily have a primary validity as quantitative evidence. Extraneous and *post hoc* methods of calculating numbers might be just as valid.

13. The best framework for such methods was the view of the whole spectrum of twentieth-century violence which was already beginning to take shape. This provided an array of comparative events and technologies which allowed one to step outside the

boundaries conventionally surrounding the study of violence, such as national myth and tradition, 'war', 'soldiers' and so on. The view of the whole offered some immediately obvious advantages. Some forms of violence such as deaths in transit or from disease amongst soldiers, which are usually marginalized by the conventional parameters, can be seen as significant in their own right in the spectrum of the whole. Hesitancy in admitting certain events because they lack credibility in the light of past experience may be overcome if similar events are confirmed as having happened elsewhere. Significant correlations may be made, as for instance between the episodes brought together under the description 'demographic violence'. And larger margins of error can be tolerated on the elevated scale achieved.

14. This elevated scale I would specifically describe as a new platform from which to view twentieth-century macro-violence. Standing on this platform, it is absolutely essential to be able to see clearly in two directions. In one direction is the particular historical period or violent episode. The specialist working in such a field still has to deal with specific sources and a mixture of precise figures and vague estimates. His task is as arduous as ever, though he may derive some support from the categories and comparisons raised by the methodology of overall analysis. This methodology, which lies in the other direction, rests on the selection of a stable order of magnitude for each major area of violence. This permits overall analysis into categories which are accurate enough to be meaningful but broadly enough based not to be too dependent on specific sources. The stability of the system lies in the fact that in any specific area a good deal of revision can occur, and a good deal of controversy over sources obtain, without affecting the validity of the overall analysis. Indeed even if the order of magnitude itself has to be revised it should not affect the overall pattern too much, since the added or subtracted number is likely to be distributed amongst different factors of analysis. One would hope that cross-fertilization between specific areas and the overall spectrum would eventually result in much finer and more sophisticated analyses than are possible in the crude system I have set up here.

15. In the next section I select an order of magnitude for each area of violence. In working to the nearest five million I am guided by the statistical feel acquired about each area, and quote the sources that have guided me. It is in no sense a rigorous examination of sources, but I have tried to summarize the main issues and in some cases to indicate the kind of demographic studies that would be necessary in order to refine the overall system. I have subjected each area to a simple set of standard analyses from which the tables and other figures used in the text are derived, and from which further tables may be culled by using the simple coding system.

16. Finally, in the table below are set out the selected orders of magnitude over the whole spectrum, together with a note as to whether the sources mainly referred to are (a) existing studies of the area; (b) mainly official sources; (c) special problem areas to which I have contributed a few suggestions.

Order of Magnitude, Major Areas of Twentieth-Century Violence

Area	Number of deaths	Type of Source
First World War	10m.	Mainly official
Russian Civil War period	10m.	Special problem
Russian Total State	20m.	Existing studies
Russia, Second World War, soldiers	10m.	Existing studies
Russia, Second World War, civilians	10m.	Special problem
The Jews of Europe	5m.	Existing studies
China, Twentieth century	20m.	Special problem
Rest of the Second World War	15m.	Mainly official
Other twentieth-century Conflicts	10m.	Mainly official

Total Estimate: 110m. *deaths*

Key to Codes Used in Standard Analyses

The raw material for overall analyses given under each area is roughly coded to help in compiling tables. Here is a guide to the categories used.

The *AREAS* themselves are numbered 1–9.

The *MAIN HEADS* used are TECHNOLOGY (meaning death technology), IDENTITY (meaning identity of victims) and

CHRONOLOGY (meaning number of deaths per annum). A system of notes and references for each item of analysis would have been more than I can manage, so the system of analysis, and any statistical weight it might have, rests on informed commonsense. I have included a few notes under Chronology since otherwise these divisions would appear rather arbitrary.

Technology

Twenty-one divisions, lettered a–u. In each case the technology, preceded by the small letter of its code, is followed by an estimate of the number of deaths, and also by a capital letter A–D signifying the category of INDIVIDUAL IDENTITY (see below) into which it falls. For example:

o. Big guns. 5m. A.

The coded technologies are now listed:

Enclosed Privation (Camp)	a. Enclosed ghetto
	b. Prisoner-of-war camp
	c. Concentration camp
	d. Labour camp
Semi-enclosed Privation (City)	e. Unenclosed ghetto
	f. Siege
	g. Occupation
	h. Civil dislocation
Diffuse Privation (Rural or mixed)	i. Transit
	j. Combat
	k. Economic blockade
	l. Man-made famine
	m. Scorched earth
	n. War dislocation
Hardware	o. Big guns
	p. Small arms – formal execution
	q. Small arms – massacre
	r. Small arms – combat
	s. Mixed – demographic
	t. Aerial bombs
Chemicals	u. Gas

Identity

Individual Identity. Three divisions – Men, Women, Children – but for analytical purposes I have in fact assigned each particular use of death technology to one of four categories of proportional split as between men, women and children. These are:

A. All men (e.g. military combat where the victims are virtually all men).
B. Men 90 per cent, women, 10 per cent (e.g. the Russian labour camps which are mainly men, but include a substantial minority of women).
C. Men 40 per cent, women 40 per cent, children 20 per cent (e.g. privation in areas where there is a normal civilian population balance).
D. Men 30 per cent, women 50 per cent, children 20 per cent (e.g. privation in civilian areas where the young men are off fighting).

A more comprehensive study would of course use these as hypotheses from which to work towards more refined categories.

Social Origin. Three divisions – Mainly peasant, Mainly urban, Mixed. This is a very crude division indeed, 'mixed' to a large extent meaning 'unassignable owing to lack of finer information'. In the text I have made a virtue of this, since the period is one of great social mobility. I do think that a really refined analysis would include some indication of the newness of urban populations.

Traditional Role. Four divisions – Peasant, Citizen, Soldier, Jew or Religious dissident.

Processed or Alienated Identity. Three divisions – Paranthropoid, Mechanthropoid, Randomized.

Chronology

I will just repeat, for the benefit of the over-enthusiastic, that my aim has not been year-by-year accuracy but a reasonable indication of rise and fall on the graph. I include the raw data because I believe in the exchange of open hypotheses as an aid to inquiry.

SOURCES AND STANDARD ANALYSES

1. First World War (mainly official sources)

The usual figure given for military deaths is $8\frac{1}{2}$ million. This was calculated by the U.S. War Department and is detailed in *Encyclopaedia Britannica* (14th edn, 1929, article on World War). Later writers have suggested 10 million or more as a truer figure. The bugbear is the concept of 'casualties' as including killed (i.e. certified as dead), died from wounds, wounded, missing and prisoners. Various of these categories are lumped together in some of the official national statistics, and we may be sure that the ranks of the official wounded and missing include many of the actual dead. I have used the figure of *9 million* as a reasonable minimum.

For civilian deaths I use the figure of *1 million*. This is based on an official German estimate of 800,000 deaths from hunger in the economic blockade of Germany, quoted by Hans Rumpf (*The Bombing of Germany* Muller, London, 1963, p. 163). Civilian deaths in other Central and Eastern European countries would bring the total up to a good deal more than that. Some writers have suggested several million civilian deaths from the overall effects of the war. The problem here is where deaths during the war merge with deaths in the long-term aftermath – a problem suitable for the kind of demographic inquiry I have suggested elsewhere.

I have not seen anywhere estimates of deaths on the different fronts. According to the U.S. War Department's analysis the proportion of Allied to Central Power deaths is precisely 3 to 2 overall. I have therefore matched Central deaths to Allied in roughly that proportion, and assigned groups of Allied nationals' deaths to three fronts. On the basis of $8\frac{1}{2}$ million adjusted to the 9 million used here, the result is:

	Number of deaths	Number of deaths	Total number
	Allied	*Central Powers* Germany, Austro-Hungary, Turkey, Bulgaria	
Western front French, British, U.S., Belgian	2·4m.	1·6m.	4m.
Italian front Italian	0·6m.	0·4m.	1m.
Eastern and Balkan fronts Russian, Rumanian, Serbian	2·5m.	1·5m.	4m.
Total	5·5m.	3·5m.	9m.

Of these, probably about a million men overall died of disease, not combat.

Standard Analysis

TECHNOLOGY

Privation

j. Combat. 1m. A.
k. Economic blockade. 1m. D.

Hardware

o. Big guns. 5m. A.
r. Small arms – combat. 3m. A.

IDENTITY

Individual Identity

A. 9m.
D. 1m.

Social Origin

Mixed. 9m.
Mainly Urban. 1m.

Traditional Role

Soldier. 9m.
Citizen. 1m.

Processed or Alienated Identity

Mechanthropoid. 9m.
Randomized. 1m.

CHRONOLOGY

1914.	1m.	Barbara Tuchman's *The Guns of August* seems to
1915.	2·5m.	suggest a level of deaths in the five months of 1914 of
1916.	2·5m.	about 1 million. 1918 – light in military deaths but
1917.	2·5m.	heavy in civilian. Heaviest battle toll 1915 and 1916
1918.	1·5m.	but I can't justify distributing over the three years
		1915–17 other than equally since the figure for 1917
		would be augmented by cumulative effects of soldier
		disease and exhaustion, deaths from wounds and
		civilian deaths.

2. *Russian Civil War Period (special problem)*

(a) *The Times* Moscow correspondent writing in 1969 gives, as the official Russian view, a figure of 14 million deaths for the period of the First World War and the Civil War. Excluding the military deaths of the world war, and the famine deaths of 1921, officially reckoned at about 1–2 million and 2–3 million respectively, I have assumed an order of magnitude of *10 million* for the actual period of the Civil War, 1917–21. This begs a number of questions. But first of all, I should like to set it alongside another calculation.

(b) Mr Ian Grey, in *The First Fifty Years, Soviet Russia 1917–67* (Hodder & Stoughton, 1967, p. 181), writes: '. . . a census conducted in 1926 accounted for a population of 147 million and, calculated on the basis of normal population growth, this figure should have been 175 million. Twenty-eight million had disappeared. The refugees from the revolution and the civil war who made their way to western Europe and to China probably numbered a million. But in the course of three-and-a-half years of war against the Central Powers and then the civil war some 27 million Russians had perished.'

It is always possible that large discrepancies between one census and another are caused by the census machinery itself. Leaving that possibility aside, the minimum discrepancy between Mr Grey's estimate and my own is as follows. Suppose deaths in the world war period to be rather larger (as is very likely), say 4 million; plus maximum 3 million deaths in 1921 famine; add my estimate of 10 million. The resultant total of 17 million is still 10 million short of Mr Grey's figure.

Now, the fact is that no proper demographic study has ever been made of the effects on population of the prolonged violent upheavals characteristic of the twentieth century. I am no demographer, but the following are some of the *possibilities* in the present case:

(i) Twelve million men served in the army in the First World War, and eventually 5 million in the Red Army. There were vast population movements between town and country, near the beginning of the Civil War and during the 1921 famine. Social disruption and separation, as in the Second World War, were of a kind not experienced in any other country and may be expected to have a very large lowering effect on the birthrate.

(ii) On the basis of 17 million deaths, if 2 or 3 million of these were women of child-bearing age, there would be a total loss of expected births before 1926 (the date of the census) amounting to several million.

(iii) Apart from this there is the simple loss of births to widowed women, and from later marriages and delayed births due to prolonged disruption.

(iv) At the other end of the life cycle: to what extent would those dying 'normally' die a year or so earlier in the aftermath of a prolonged period of hardship and insecurity? How many 'years off your life' does such a period take?

If there is a substantial phenomenon of this nature it would have the effect on census data of 'bringing foward' a large number of expected normal deaths by a year or so.

Could such factors account for the discrepancy of 10 million?

(c) Until the demographic factors are properly studied we must leave the question open, and I have taken 10 million as a minimal basis to the detailed estimates made in the text.

Standard Analysis

TECHNOLOGY

Privation

---

h. Civil dislocation. 8m. C.

Hardware

---

r. Small arms – combat. 1m. A.
s. Mixed – demographic. 1m. B.

IDENTITY

Individual Identity

A. 1m.
B. 1m.
C. 8m.

Social Origin

Mainly peasant. 1m.
Mainly urban. 8m.
Mixed. 1m.

Traditional Role

Peasant. 1m.
Citizen. 8m.
Soldier. 1m.

Processed or Alienated Identity

Mechanthropoid. 1m.
Randomized. 9m.

CHRONOLOGY

1917.	1m.	One can only distribute this according to the general
1918.	3m.	pattern of peak violence and privation in 1918–19, with
1919.	3m.	the cumulative effects stretching up to 1921. Discussed
1920.	2m.	in Chapter 3.
1921.	1m.	

3. Russian Total State (existing studies)

The best collation of sources is in Robert Conquest's *The Great Terror* and I am dependent upon his arguments for the order of magnitude of 20 million deaths as 'the price of Stalin'. It is quite appropriate in this field I think to accept the same order of magnitude while offering somewhat different hypotheses as to detailed analyses. In this case they arise from a different historical perspective. Mr Conquest's focal point is the series of political purges of the 1930s. My own concern is the scale of violence over the whole period, and for this reason it seems necessary to emphasize the collectivization as the first great violent episode engineered by the new state. The main divisions I have used are as follows:

Collectivization:

Man-made famine	5m.	
Killing and privation	2m.	
Camps	3m.	*Total 10m.*

Other forms of violence:

Camps	9m.	
Shot in prisons	1m.	*Total 10m.*

Mr Conquest does not suggest an actual figure for 'killing and privation', by which I mean the direct killing operations and the accompanying deaths from privation on the farm and in transit. But since this is the very core of the collectivization violence it seems necessary to make an attempt to quantify it. This is the nearest order of magnitude I can imagine from the accounts I have read, none of which seem to have much understanding of what actually happened. The figure for 'shot in prisons' is taken from

Mr Conquest. So is the figure for 'Man-made famine', although I am not clear how far he has included this in his final total; if he has partly left it out it would explain why his figure for deaths in the camps seems to be about 15 million against my 12 million. However, 12 and 15 million are about equally valid on the basis of his arguments. The last phase of the Stalinist labour camps has not I believe been put in perspective by anyone yet, and the final number who died remains a very open question. The fact is that the 20 million estimate for this whole period may well be a conservative order of magnitude. Those who still believe it is exaggerated must read Appendix A of *The Great Terror* and if necessary the further sources quoted by Mr Conquest ... or alternatively of course, continue to believe it is exaggerated ...

Standard Analysis

TECHNOLOGY

Privation

---

d. Labour camps.   12m.   B.
i. Transit.   1m.   C.
l. Man-made famine.   5m.   C.

Hardware

---

p. Small arms – formal execution.   1m.   A.
q. Small arms – massacre.   1m.   A.

IDENTITY

Individual Identity

A. 2m.
B. 12m.
C. 6m.

Social Origin

Mainly peasant.   10m.
Mainly urban.   10m.

Traditional Role

Peasant.	10m.
Citizen.	8m.
Soldier.	1m.
Religious dissident.	1m.

Processed or Alienated Identity

Paranthropoid.	20m.

CHRONOLOGY

1930.	1m.	To attempt a chronology here is almost hope-
1931.	1m.	less but I have indicated two definite peaks –
1932.	3m.	the collectivization killings and deportations
1933.	3m.	from 1930 culminating in the man-made
1934.	1m.	famine of 1932–3 with peasants continuing to
1935.	1m.	die in the labour camps for the next few years;
1936.	1m.	and then the terror years of 1936–8. In the
1937.	2m.	later years there may be peaks that it is not yet
1938.	1m.	possible to discern, and the estimates for the
1939–50.		rest of the period may of course only be half
incl.	0·5m. p.a.	of the truth.

4. *Russia: Second World War, Soldiers (existing studies)*

The Russian official figure for all war deaths, civilian and military, is 20 million. No breakdowns are given. There is no reason to doubt the magnitude of this figure, and most commentators if anything consider it an underestimate. The most reasonable basis I have been able to find for analysis is to suggest an order of magnitude of 10 million civilian and 10 million military deaths, and to discuss each within these limits.

For the military campaigns I have used Alexander Werth, *Russia at War* (Barrie & Rockliff, 1964). This book follows the campaigns closely and gives, close to the battle themselves and with periodic summaries, the best figures available. The best figures are not a great help in arriving at a final total, but they indicate (especially the figures of German losses) the relative magnitude of loss as one follows the patterns of the war.

The order of magnitude of 10 million lies between the two major estimates I have considered. Werth suggests 'at least

7 million deaths'. A German statistical study quoted in Hanson Baldwin, *Battles Lost and Won*, gives analysis which would lead to a conclusion of 13·6 million deaths. I am sceptical of 'statistical studies' since statisticians, like historians, rely a great deal on something called 'documentary evidence' which is a very limited indicator of reality. I have seen similarly high figures cited by American writers without indicating sources. An exact source is highly improbable. Military intelligence, for example, would be about as credible as, say, an NKVD man's estimate of the labour camp population, some of which exist but are not considered particularly authoritative. However, lending some credence to the higher figure, we arrive at the following comparison of estimates lightly analysed:

German Study		Werth		Estimate used	
8·5m.	action or missing	3·0m.	action	5·0m.	action
2·5m.	wounds	1·0m.	wounds	2·0m.	wounds, disease, cold
2·6m.	p.o.w. camps	3·0m.	p.o.w. camps	3·0m.	p.o.w. camps

The prisoner-of-war camp deaths are separately analysed in Werth.

Standard Analysis

TECHNOLOGY

Privation

b. Prisoner-of-war camp. 3m. A.

Hardware

o. Big guns. 5m. A. r. Small arms – combat. 2m. A.

IDENTITY

Individual Identity

A. 10m.

Social Origin

Mainly peasants. 10m.

Traditional Role

Soldier. 10m.

Processed or Alienated Identity

Paranthropoid. 3m.
Mechanthropoid. 7m.

CHRONOLOGY

1941.	2m.	This is based on a calculation of the density of combat
1942.	3m.	deaths over the period as well as the rate of prisoner
1943.	2·5m.	deaths and the probable rate of deaths from wounds.
1944.	1·5m.	
1945.	1m.	

5. *Russia: Second World War, Civilians* (*special problem*)

Given an order of magnitude of 10 million deaths (see preceding section) the question is how they analyse into types of death. My method of doing this is exposed in the text. Most of the material revealing the scale of operations, the extent of hard violence wreaked on civilians, the population losses in cities during the war, is scattered throughout Werth's *Russia at War*. A great many exercises of comparing this material, of considering the realistic scale on which different types of violence operate, and so on, have led me to the particular shape of the pyramid on page 58.

I should mention that the Jews massacred in Russia are also included in the computation of the Jews of Europe. Since we are dealing in orders of magnitude, overlaps of this kind have no statistical significance.

Standard Analysis

TECHNOLOGY

Privation

f. Siege. 1m. D.
g. Occupation. 5m. D.
m. Scorched earth. 1m. D.

Hardware

p. Small arms – formal execution. 0·5m. A.
q. Small arms – massacre. 2m. C.
r. Small arms – combat. 0·5m. A.

IDENTITY

Individual Identity

A. 1m.
C. 2m.
D. 7m.

Social Origin

Mainly peasant. 2m.
Mainly urban. 8m.

Traditional Role

Peasant. 2m.
Citizen. 8m.

Processed or Alienated Identity

Randomized. 10m.

CHRONOLOGY

1941. 0·5m. This is based on calculations of the rate of various
1942. 2·5m. kinds of pressure, and a suggestion of substantial
1943. 3m. deaths in the aftermath of actual pressure – 1945 and
1944. 2m. 1946.
1945. 1m.
1946. 1m.

6. *China in the Twentieth Century* (*special problem*)

My estimates are based first on sporadic readings in sources
such as Edgar Snow, *Red Star Over China*; Agnes Smedley, *The
Great Road*; Chalmers Johnson, *Peasant Nationalism and
Communist Power*; Stuart Schram, *Mao Tse-Tung*; the Pelican
China Readings; and the celebrated *Fan-Shen*.

My impression from these, and from contacts with the
Chinese Studies departments of two universities, one in England

and one in America, is that there exists little sense of an overall scale of violence in China over the whole period, and that it would be quite impossible to verify some of the rather bold estimates that I made from first impressions. I have therefore concentrated on importing a modest degree of perspective into the subject.

Phase 1: I have seen this in the light of the remarks I made on public terror in the chapter on the Russian Civil War period.

Phase 2: Edgar Snow suggests about a million peasants died in Kiangsi. Agnes Smedley suggests many privation deaths in the course of the Long March. But for calculation purposes I use a figure of one million deaths for the pre-1937 period.

Phases 3 and 4: The American university helpfully suggested that the estimates of 6–10 million deaths for the Sino-Japanese war, which I had seen in various places, might be an underestimate for a country already on the edge of subsistence. I have therefore suggested 10 million for slow privation over all China. The estimate of 5 million for hard violence and immediate privation is based on impressions I derived from Chalmers Johnson, who discusses the Japanese scorched earth policy in North China, from *China Readings*, which cover the war in South China, and from *Fan-Shen*, which brings home the effect in the villages.

The other estimates are I think fairly widely accepted apart from that for 'demographic violence' which is my own speculation.

Standard Analysis

TECHNOLOGY

Privation

m. Scorched earth. 4m. D.
n. War dislocation. 10m. C.

Hardware

o. Big guns. 1m. A.
p. Small arms – formal execution. 2m. A.
q. Small arms – massacre. 1m. B.
r. Small arms – combat. 1m. A.
s. Mixed – demographic. 1m. B.

IDENTITY

Individual Identity

A. 4m.
B. 2m.
C. 10m.
D. 4m.

Social Origin

Mainly peasant. 17m.
Mixed. 3m.

Traditional Role

Peasant. 14m.
Citizen. 4m.
Soldier. 2m.

Processed or Alienated Identity

Paranthropoid. 3m.
Mechanthropoid. 2m.
Randomized. 15m.

CHRONOLOGY

1933. 0·5m. ⎫ pre-war	1941. 3m. ⎫ Peaks of 3-all policy,
1934. 0·5m. ⎭	1942. 3m. ⎬ scorched earth, famine,
1937. 1m.	1943. 3m. ⎭ cumulative privation.
1938. 1m.	1944. 1m.
1939. 1m.	1945. 1m.
1940. 1m.	1946. 1m.
	1947. 0·5m.
	1948. 0·5m.
	1951. 2m. Executions.

7. The Jews of Europe (existing studies)

For the Jews of Europe I have used Gerald Reitlinger's *The
Final Solution*. His total figure is 4·25 million deaths. I have
used the figure of 5 million deaths, including 1 million Russian
Jews although his figure is somewhat less than that. The main
area of discrepancy is amongst the large numbers of Polish Jews
who fled into Russia at the beginning of the war and whose fate

is unknown. I have used a number of figures collated from Mr Reitlinger's book and give these as they stand. My use of the larger figure of 5 million is in deference to the phenomenon of people who slip through, not only official estimates but the most meticulous attempts at unofficial estimates. There are of course many sources for the Jewish deaths, but Mr Reitlinger's is the most definitive one and establishes a minimal figure with very little doubt.

Standard Analysis

TECHNOLOGY

Privation

a. Enclosed ghetto.   1m.   C.
c. Concentration camp.   0·5m.   C.
e. Unenclosed ghetto.   1m.   C.

Hardware

q. Small arms – massacre.   1m.   C.

Chemicals

u. Gas.   1·5m.   C.

IDENTITY

Individual Identity

C. 5m.

Social Origin

Mainly urban.   5m.

Traditional Role

Jew.   5m.

Processed or Alienated Identity

Paranthropoid.   5m.

CHRONOLOGY

1941.	0·5m.	So far as I am aware this roughly follows the indica-
1942.	2·5m.	tions suggested by Mr Reitlinger's book, but it is my
1943.	1·5m.	own chronology.
1944.	0·5m.	

8. *The Rest of the Second World War (mainly official sources)*

The estimate of 15 million deaths is probably the most reliable of all those given, mainly because they are the collected statistics of twenty different nations. I have taken them from a list compiled by Hanson Baldwin in his book *Battles Lost and Won* (Hodder & Stoughton, 1967).

The only cases where there is likely to be a large discrepancy are those of Germany and Poland. German military statistics broke down at the end of January 1945 when the country was being overrun, and the figure up to then was 2 million military deaths. The official estimate is 4 million. This is explained by the large numbers killed in the last months of the war, plus at least a million sent to Russian prison camps who did not return. Half a million Germans died in Allied bombing raids. There is also a figure of 2 million 'missing in mass migration or flight'. Given the disorder in Germany at the end of the war it must be presumed a large proportion of these died in conditions of privation. I have presumed half a million, although I have seen another estimate of 1·2 million (I find it difficult to believe such a precise estimate). At any rate the figure of 5 million deaths overall in Germany is likely to be accurate within a million either way.

The Polish figures are problematical. The estimate of around half a million for combat death, both civil and military, makes sense given the brief, devastating combat period that began the Second World War, and the Warsaw uprising at the end of it. So does the figure of half a million dying from wounds and malnutrition, given the fiercely depressed condition of Poland under German occupation. But the figure of 1·6 million deaths in camps is a puzzle, since the Poles do not seem to distinguish between Jewish and non-Jewish deaths in camps. On the other hand, it seems that of one million Poles shipped to Russian labour camps after the Russian attack of 1939, at least a quarter died there. It seems the correct figure must be somewhere between 1½ million and 3 million non-Jewish Poles. I have used the figure of 3 million, although this may be exaggerated.

Standard Analysis

TECHNOLOGY

Privation

b. Prisoner-of-war camp. 1·5m. A.
c. Concentration camp. 2m. B.
g. Occupation. 1m. C.
i. Transit. 0·5m. C.

Hardware

o. Big guns. 5m. A.
p. Small arms – formal execution. 0·5m. A.
r. Small arms – combat. 3·5m. A.
t. Aerial bombs. 1m. D.

IDENTITY

Individual Identity

A. 10·5m.
B. 2m.
C. 1·5m.
D. 1m.

Social Origin

Mixed. 15m.

Traditional Role

Citizen. 5m.
Soldier. 10m.

Processed or Alienated Identity

Paranthropoid. 3·5m.
Mechanthropoid. 8·5m.
Randomized. 3m.

CHRONOLOGY

1940.	2m.	1943.	3m.
1941.	3m.	1944.	2m.
1942.	3m.	1945.	2m.

9. *Other Twentieth-Century Conflicts (mainly official sources)*

The obvious question here is comprehensiveness. However, to put the matter in perspective, it should be remembered that, if a 'small' conflict is one in which up to a thousand lives are lost, one would have to have missed out a thousand of such conflicts to be in error by one million. So the question comes back to the validity of the larger areas of violence.

Indian Partition deaths have been estimated at between 1 and 2 million, as have deaths in the *Nigerian Civil War* (Biafra). In both cases I have taken the lower figure. It only recently came to my attention (through *Revolution! Mexico 1910–20*, Ronald Atkin, Macmillan, 1969) that 2 million died in the *Mexican Revolution* and I have looked at other areas of violence over the twentieth century for similar hidden areas.

The main possibilities of large-scale deaths are South America, Africa in the immediate post-colonial phase, and South-East Asia (civilians) since the end of the Second World War. The African conflicts though usually of great political significance have seldom been on a large physical scale apart from the one I have mentioned. In the case of South America I have assumed that most of the recurrent upheavals take the shapes of civil violence, that is, not large armed conflicts, and are not disruptive enough to cause widespread hardship, being mostly in the cities and those in peasant areas being of a small nature. As to South-East Asia, we do have estimates for civilian deaths there but their final accuracy would be doubtful. The effects of macro-violence on civil life there would at present be the subject of intensive study with a £50m. budget, if there were any real priorities in the world of study.

Standard Analysis

TECHNOLOGY

Privation

k. Economic blockade. 1m. C.
n. War dislocation. 2m. C.

Hardware

o. Big guns. 2m. A.
q. Small arms – massacre. 1m. C.
r. Small arms – combat. 3m. A.
s. Mixed – demographic. 1m. B.

IDENTITY

Individual Identity

A. 5m.
B. 1m.
C. 4m.

Social Origin

Mainly peasant. 3m.
Mixed. 7m.

Traditional Role

Peasant. 3m.
Citizen. 2m.
Soldier. 5m.

Processed or Alienated Identity

Mechanthropoid. 5m.
Randomized. 5m.

CHRONOLOGY

1912. 0·5m.	1930. 0·5m.	1951. 0·5m.
1914. 1m.	1931. 0·5m.	1952. 0·5m.
1915. 0·5m.	1936. 0·5m.	1955. 0·5m.
1918. 1m.	1939. 0·5m.	1967. 0·5m.
1920. 0·5m.	1947. 1m.	1968. 1m.
1921. 0·5m.		

Distributed somewhat more spikily than they occurred in actuality.

INDEX

INDEX

UNLESS PEACE COMES

A Scientific Forecast of New Weapons

Edited by Nigel Calder

Unless Peace Comes is a calm appraisal of the future of atomic, biological and chemical weapons (fondly termed ABC) and other possible developments in warfare. The contributors are no bunch of bearded idealists: they are experts and scientists of world reputation – men of the calibre of General Beaufre, the French director of strategic studies, Professor Gordon Macdonald, the American geophysicist, and the late Sir John Cockcroft. In the coming armoury of destruction to which they give sober consideration are cobalt bombs, infectious clouds, psychic poisons, and robot armies (not to mention tidal waves).

The space devoted by the press to the grim contents of this book, when it was published by Allen Lane The Penguin Press, is evidence enough of its public interest and importance. As Neville Brown wrote in the *New Scientist*: 'There has long been a need . . . for a text that discusses the evolution of military techniques in terms that the interested layman finds neither depressingly esoteric nor maddeningly simple: and this is what Mr Calder and his colleagues have succeeded in providing.'

THE WORLD IN 1984

(in two volumes)

Edited by Nigel Calder

New Scientist achieved what must rank as one of the most extraordinary publishing coups of this century, when it commissioned almost a hundred leading international authorities in many different fields literally to look into the future. The result was a series of articles as fascinating as the best science fiction shorn of the fantasy.

The World in 1984 brings these articles together in two volumes. In an effort to forecast accurately future developments, they look beyond science and technology to politics, trade, the arts, and other fields. Their intention is entirely serious – to build up as true a picture of the world in 1984 as the best information of today will allow.

Here, filled out with facts, is 'the prophetic soul of the wide world, dreaming on things to come.'

Volume 1 includes contributions by Lord Todd, Sir John Cockcroft, Dr Wernher von Braun, Professor Fred Hoyle, and Professor John Yudkin.

Volume 2 includes contributions by Joan Littlewood, Professor Asa Briggs, Barbara Wootton, Professor B. F. Skinner, Professor Richard Hoggart and Lord Brain.